"What a wise, practical, so very helpful book Ryan P. Tinetti has given us in *The Quiet Ambition*. He moves so gracefully from the words of Saint Paul to the stresses and strains of contemporary life, giving us practical ways in which each of us can be faithful to the use of the gifts God has given us without allowing our ambition and drive to get the best of us. In reading, I constantly said, 'This book was written for me.' I bet that you will find it was written for you too."

Will Willimon, professor of the practice of Christian ministry at Duke Divinity School and author of *Accidental Preacher: A Memoir*

"In a world of constant motion and noise, Ryan P. Tinetti offers a refreshing invitation to a different way of living—one that leads not only to a deeper understanding of ourselves but also of God. *The Quiet Ambition* is a guiding light for those feeling restless and weary from life's relentless demands, showing a path to true purpose and peace. I wish I had read this book years ago, but as Ryan reminds us, it's never too late to 'make it your ambition to live quietly.'"

Tanner Olson, writer at writtentospeak.com

"'Unambitious ambition' is Ryan P. Tinetti's hope-filled response to the gnawing fear of failing to do great things for God. Drawing on many years of pastoral ministry and seminary teaching, Tinetti squarely addresses us in our exhaustion, burnout, or perhaps embarrassment about our lack of accomplishment. *The Quiet Ambition* offers an extended meditation on Paul's encouragement to live quietly (1 Thess. 4:11-12). This is a book filled to the brim with practical words of wisdom to be chewed and savored."

Hans Boersma, professor at Nashotah House Theological Seminary in Wisconsin and author of *Pierced by Love*

"In North America, ambition has become an object of hope, and paradoxically, a source of despair, resignation, and hopelessness. Yet rather than attacking ambition, Ryan P. Tinetti places it in its proper place, not as a replacement for our hope in the newness of life but as its servant. With theological depth and pastoral wisdom, the author invites weary and withdrawn souls to see the great things God is already doing to make all things new as his Spirit channels our holy desires for Christlike service through our little, everyday tasks and quiet, unassuming lives. A hope-filled book!"

Leopoldo A. Sánchez M., professor of systematic theology at Concordia Seminary and author of *Sculptor Spirit*

"Ryan P. Tinetti opens our eyes to the glories of the simple, common, and ordinary—where God's highest and best work is done by the lowliest people. Laced copiously with captivating illustrations from books, media, culture, and his own sensitive ministry among God's simple saints, Tinetti skillfully weaves the thread of God's riches at Christ's expense throughout. A call to slow down and live more calmly for Jesus."

Harold Senkbeil, author of *The Care of Souls* and executive director of DOXOLOGY: The Lutheran Center for Spiritual Care and Counsel

"The apostle Paul directs his readers to 'encourage one another and build each other up,' which is exactly what Ryan P. Tinetti's new book will do for those weary with a religious culture driven by spiritual ambitions. Drawing on a range of wisdom from Scripture, history, and pastoral experience, Tinetti's book is the guide we all need to the peace that passes all ambition. This is a saving message."

Richard Lischer, James T. and Alice Mead Cleland Professor Emeritus of Preaching at Duke Divinity School and author of *Our Hearts Are Restless*

"This timely book is 'for those who have not done great things,' which is to say, most of us. It charts a better way to live for Christ without adding busy activities to the tyranny of our overloaded schedules. It all starts with an apparently humdrum verse: 'Make it your ambition to live quietly, tend your own business, and work with your hands' (1 Thess 4:11). Here is a tract for our burnout times. What really matters to Jesus, Ryan P. Tinetti suggests, is attending faithfully to our simple quotidian responsibilities, quietly witnessing to the sufficient grace of Christ."

Sylvie Vanhoozer, author of *The Art of Living in Season* and *The Art of Living in Advent*

"Using the wisdom of a scholar, the insight of a pastor, and the practicality of a husband and father, Ryan P. Tinetti sheds bright but warm and tender light on the underappreciated and often maligned path of unambitious ambition. With disarming wit and deft argument, *The Quiet Ambition* challenges a world and church still thoroughly infected by the criteria of total work to consider the goodness and beauty of a humble and unpretentious life of faithfully following Christ."

Joel Biermann, Waldemar A. and June Schuette Professor of Systematic Theology at Concordia Seminary

"I love how Ryan P. Tinetti writes—there is an almost poetic lilt to his prose. And I love what Ryan writes—insight, wisdom, humor, and hope all wrapped around a holy, biblical core. Thank you, Ryan, for *The Quiet Ambition*. It is what we all need and how we all need it."

Greg Finke, author of the Joining Jesus series

"Numerous resources help people build back their faith when broken by failure. Ryan P. Tinetti tackles an opposite crisis: how achievement can also break church workers, especially as we lionize leaders with a celebrity-like limelight. A veritable overachiever himself, Tinetti is well-qualified to address success's meretricious traps. Self-effacingly confessing his own fumbles and stumbles, Tinetti offers biblically anchored insights from an ecumenical array of theological thinkers, spiritual writers, and cultural observers. Tinetti's insights refresh the Christian tradition with practical wisdom."

John A Nunes, president of California Lutheran University

"I can think of few more pressing spiritual concerns in the age of the influencer—both inside and outside the church—than that of ambition. Fortunately, I can think of few guides more suited to this thorny terrain than Ryan P. Tinetti. *The Quiet Ambition* abounds with practical wisdom, timeless insight, and infectious humility. It's also extraordinarily well-written and funny. I have no doubt that a great many people, myself included, will benefit enormously."

David Zahl, author of *Seculosity* and *The Big Relief*

"Reading *The Quiet Ambition* is like sitting across the table from a pastor who gets it. Ryan P. Tinetti doesn't peddle the usual moralistic drivel or self-help formulas masquerading as theology. He steps into the quiet despair so many of us carry—the feeling that our lives might not matter—and he speaks the gospel straight into it. With a voice that is both biblical and pastoral, Tinetti reminds us that our hope is not in doing great things for God but in Christ, who has done it for us. This book is real theology clothed in everyday life."

Scott L. Keith, executive director of 1517

THE QUIET AMBITION

Scripture's Surprising Antidote
to Our Restless Lives

Ryan P. Tinetti

An imprint of InterVarsity Press
Downers Grove, Illinois

InterVarsity Press
P.O. Box 1400 | Downers Grove, IL 60515-1426
ivpress.com | email@ivpress.com

InterVarsity Press® is the publishing division of InterVarsity Christian Fellowship/USA®. For more information, visit intervarsity.org.

Published in association with The Bindery Agency, www.TheBinderyAgency.com.

Cover design: Faceout Studio, Spencer Fuller
Interior design: Jeanna Wiggins
Cover image: © Tim Macpherson / Stone via Getty Images

ISBN 978-1-5140-1189-8 (print) | ISBN 978-1-5140-1190-4 (digital)

Printed in the United States of America ♾

Library of Congress Cataloging-in-Publication Data
A catalog record for this book is available from the Library of Congress.

31 30 29 28 27 26 25 | 12 11 10 9 8 7 6 5 4 3 2 1

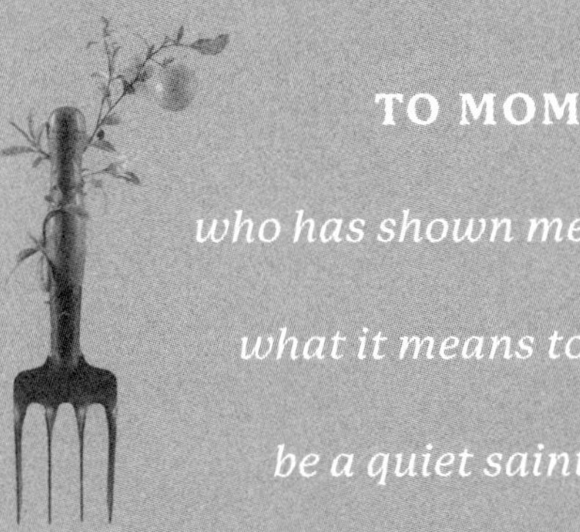

TO MOM,

who has shown me

what it means to

be a quiet saint

CONTENTS

PREFACE

THIS BOOK WAS CONCEIVED in the parish and brought forth in the seminary. Across two decades I have served the church in a range of roles: as an overseas missionary, as a church planter, and then for fourteen years as a parish pastor. I've lived in urban, suburban, and rural small-town settings, served at small and midsize churches, with multiple staffs and all by my lonesome. My ministry bingo card is pretty full.

Now I have the privilege to teach at a seminary, where our mission is to form pastors and other leaders for the church. My days are given to reflecting on and imparting the art of pastoral ministry and the craft of communicating the good news. It's at this convergence of experience and reflection, of practicing and pondering, that this book is born.

What motivates the book is a disheartening pattern I have noticed among those I have walked alongside throughout my ministry; I've noticed it in myself too. Over and again, I've seen and heard how the people of God wonder whether (or how) their lives—seemingly so small and insignificant—could have eternal and lasting significance. *What difference can my little life have on this huge world?!* More poignant still, those paper cuts to the soul start to bleed out hopefulness. Such conversations typically end in prayer and tears, both for the parishioner and the pastor.

Now I help to form the pastors who go out to minister to such folks. But not only do their parishioners feel at times insignificant and small; the pastors themselves suffer it too. A handful make it to megachurches and so-called Significant Ministries, but the majority will tend the Lord's vineyard in out-of-the-way places, with congregations that can't fill their pews, whose best days seem to be behind them. Such is ministry in twenty-first-century North America.

People respond differently to these conditions, as I'll describe further in chapter one. To oversimplify, I see largely two reactions to this perceived inadequacy and inferiority, which are two sides of the same coin. The one is what I call *restless* ambition: the kind of hustle culture, ladder climbing that we've become all too familiar with in the age of exhibitionist social media. The other, less well known but arguably even more lethal, is *resigned* ambition. It either outright rejects ambition or else despairs of it. This happens when people check out of life, figuratively or—all too often—literally.[1]

But there's a better way. One that honors the God-given drive to exercise our gifts well in service to others, without allowing that drive to take us over the cliff. It's a way that I have witnessed among countless Christians through the years (many of whom themselves don't realize they're doing it), a way that, when we have eyes to see, we start to recognize being lived out all over the place—often without remark or acclaim.

I call it the quiet ambition. It's encapsulated in a sneaky-good little verse from 1 Thessalonians: "Make it your ambition to live quietly, tend your own business, and work with your hands, so that you walk gracefully toward outsiders and have need of nothing" (1 Thess 4:11-12).[2] In this book, I'll show how this verse doesn't just offer moral instruction or doctrinal truth; it points us toward a pathway to hope that takes shape in everyday life. For that's what the Bible, and God's good news that is whispered on every page, finally has as its aim: that "through the encouragement of the Scriptures we might have hope" (Rom 15:4).

And this brings me to why I write this book and whom I write it for.

For Those Who Haven't Done "Great Things" for God

A few years back a remarkable book came out called *Every Moment Holy*.[3] Authored by Douglas McKelvey, it's a collection of "liturgies" (responsive prayers) for the ordinary events of everyday life. There are liturgies for the washing of windows and the planting of flowers, for the first hearth fire of the season and for the changing of diapers (not one but two such liturgies—so many diapers). It's a lovely book that I have found both personally and pastorally enriching.

But there's one liturgy that especially struck me: "A Liturgy for Those Who Have *Not* Done Great Things for God." In it the petitioner asks,

> How many times have I been told,
> O Christ, by well-meaning people,
> that it is my destiny and my charge
> to go out into the world
> and do great things for you?[4]

Don't waste your life! Make it count! Leave your mark and multiply those talents! And when you don't—or when, at any rate, it *feels* like you don't—what then? Thus the prayer continues,

> How many times have I felt then
> the gradually settling weight of disillusionment,
> of disappointment and confusion,
> when no *great thing* materialized, when no

> life-changing opportunity suddenly
> arrived at my doorstep, when no such moment
> of call or clarity was ever manifest at all?

This is the crux. This is when frustrated hopes take their toll and disillusionment starts to settle in. So the petitioner laments,

> I am faced again
> with the same litany of tired,
> old temptations
> towing their attendant shames,
> and in such times I am left, O Lord,
> wondering if I have somehow
> missed your call completely,
> and whether I might just as well abandon
> this pilgrim path entirely,
> for I fear that you must see me as I see myself:
> unfit
> for any service to you,
> or to your people,
> or to this world.[5]

You can hear in this plaintive confession the stakes of the matter. They're what compel my writing of this book.

I'm writing it for those who think they have *not* done great things for God, who want their lives to mean something, who want to use their talents well but who fear that their efforts can never amount to much. For exhausted caretakers and burned-out homemakers; for the blue-collar believer who is a bit embarrassed to admit that he happens to *like* unclogging toilets for people and for the white-collar Christian who wants to keep his foot on the pedal without it always being to the floor (and maybe find the brake too); for small church pastors who aren't changing the world and for suburban dads who are toiling at a job they don't love because they believe their primary vocation is to provide for their family; for college grads wondering what's next; and for country kids wondering what now.

But as I teach my students in preaching courses, every sermon also starts with pastors preaching to themselves. And so this book is unmistakably for me too. I write not as a self-assured expert but as a fellow stumbling traveler on this hopeful journey of life in Christ. I'm thus writing for all those who, like me, long for nothing more than to hear, when it's all said and done, "Well done, good and faithful servant! Enter into the joy of your master!"

The liturgy from *Every Moment Holy* has a responding voice of grace. It says,

> Tend well those things
> that are before you, however humble they be,
> and he will lead you in time
> to other good works he has appointed for you.
> Whether big or small is of no matter.
> He attaches no numbers
> to your service. It is your heart
> and faithfulness he appraises.[6]

This is the message of the quiet ambition. It's a message of hope for everyday life, a message that finds the largeness in littleness. In a world that (as one writer famously said) persists in the thrall of "quiet desperation," it may be just the message we need.

Part 1

MAKE IT YOUR AMBITION

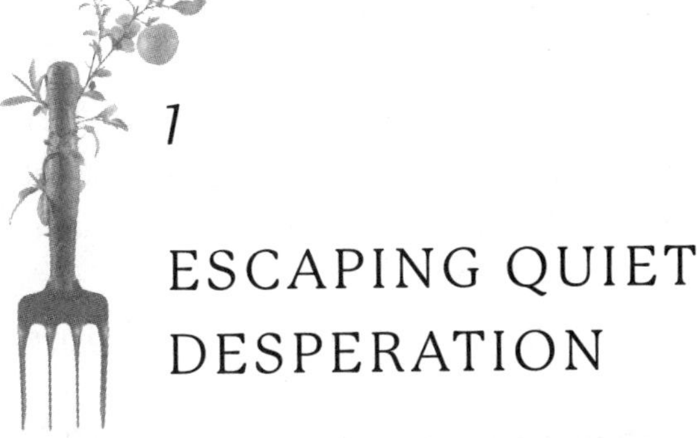

1

ESCAPING QUIET DESPERATION

On the Fourth of July, in the year of our Lord 1845, shouting distance from the "shot heard 'round the world" that birthed the American Revolution, as modern industry took hold and the fruits of Enlightenment ambitions thrummed and buzzed all around him, Henry David Thoreau moved into the woods.

In keeping with the nature of the holiday, he was staging a kind of protest. Drawing a line in the sand of existence, if you will.[1] He had good reason to do so. While his writing often reached to exalted heights, Thoreau's everyday life had fallen down in the dumps. After graduating from Harvard, he ran through a series of jobs: teacher, surveyor, pencil maker (the family business). Whispers about whether he would make something of himself were not unfounded.

More recently, Thoreau's name had become a byword in his small Concord community. He's famous as a naturalist now, but in 1844 a campfire gone horribly wrong turned into a wildfire that destroyed some three hundred acres of the last remaining virgin woodlands surrounding the town. Neighbors taunted him for years afterwards as the "woods-burner."[2]

Then there was the shadow of Henry's brother and best friend, John. His first full day taking residence at Walden, July 5th, would have been John's thirty-first birthday. Three years prior, however, John cut his finger sharpening a razor. Shortly thereafter, a lethal case of lockjaw set in, and in a matter of days John died a painful death cradled in Henry's arms.[3]

Thoreau therefore lodged his protest with existence by lodging in the woods. He was embarking on a quest to "live deliberately" and determine whether his life, already at twenty-eight so full of contradictory clues, might mean anything—or, he says, "If it proved to be mean, why then to get the whole and genuine meanness of it, and publish its meanness to the world."[4]

"Thoreau wanted to make his life matter," says the great historian David McCullough. "That's a very big lesson for all of us to keep in mind: to make your life matter. To walk off stage having done something that's beneficial, encouraging, stimulating, or inspiring."[5]

In doing so, Thoreau sought to counteract a grave threat. Given some of the trials he had already encountered, it was surely a threat that he sensed lurking at his own door. A keen people-watcher, though, he detected its presence pervading society:

> The mass of men lead lives of quiet desperation. What is called resignation is confirmed desperation. From the desperate city you go into the desperate country and have to console yourself with the bravery of minks and muskrats. A stereotyped but unconscious despair is concealed even under what are called the games and amusements of mankind.[6]

Quiet desperation. A bone-chilling phrase, that. Thoreau doesn't bother to define it, and maybe he doesn't need to. I've come to think of it as the slow seeping of hope. The Latin *desperare* means literally to be "devoid of hope." But quiet desperation doesn't set in with one decisive step, like the damned passing beneath the gates of Dante's *Inferno*: "Abandon all hope, ye who enter here." It's more like quicksand: you gradually seep into its clutches, inch by unconscious inch, until it's too late to escape. Or as C. S. Lewis describes "the safest road to Hell" in *The Screwtape Letters*: the quicksand of quiet desperation claims its victims by means of "the gentle slope, soft underfoot, without sudden turnings, without milestones, without signposts."[7]

I believe that quiet desperation sets in when there's a disconnect between desires and reality, ambitions and actualities. As a pastor, I have occasion to conduct marriage counseling with couples. One thing that I warn them about is what I call the Zone of Frustration. The Zone of Frustration, I say, is the chasm that opens up when there's a gap between the expectations you have of your spouse and the person that he or she actually is (for better or for worse, you might say). When that chasm grows too great, mere frustration can morph into quiet desperation, and you lose hope for your relationship. This can happen in your relationship with your spouse, but I believe that it can also happen in your relationship to your life—and, indeed, to God. But I'm getting ahead of myself.

In Thoreau's day, he witnessed quiet desperation in the frantic toil of businessmen and the beleaguered forbearance of housewives. He observed it in people who were passing through their days the way they passed by the countryside in the newfangled railcars. "Our inventions are wont to be pretty toys, which distract our attention from serious things," he writes. "They are but improved means to an unimproved end, an end which it was already but too easy to arrive at; as railroads lead to Boston or New York."[8]

Restlessness and Resignation

Are things any better in the twenty-first century? To the contrary, it seems that quiet desperation has spread like a river that has overrun its banks. If it was seeping in when Thoreau moved to

Walden, now it's spilling over every plain and plateau. There's barely a solid place to stand. And in our day quiet desperation manifests itself in a pair of seemingly opposite responses: *restless ambition* and *resigned ambition*.

Restless ambition is desperate busyness. It's the anxious drive to do more, get more, be more. The supposition, more assumed than asserted, is that some ingenuity and good old can-do attitude can stave off that awful sinking feeling. Restlessness is reflected in recent years, for instance, in the rise of what's been called "hustle culture." Also known as "toil glamour" (who's coming up with this stuff?), hustle culture lionizes overwork and thanks God when it's Monday (T.G.I.M.). It boasts in skipping breaks and leaving leisure behind.

There are impressive facets to this attitude. Restless ambition is characteristically American, if not uniquely so, and it has certainly had a hand in the prosperity of our country. As Alexander Hamilton sings in the song "My Shot" from the insanely popular musical *Hamilton: An American Musical*, "Hey yo, I'm just like my country / I'm young, scrappy and hungry."[9] Restlessness is how many Americans roll, and we all benefit from it.

There's undeniably a dark side to restless ambition, however. You can see it in dramatic fashion in the documentary *Conan O'Brien Can't Stop*, which follows the comedian on tour after he left the *Tonight Show*. It's at times humorous, but ultimately poignant as we witness O'Brien struggling with his need to keep on pushing ahead to wow the next crowd, to get the next laugh. At one point, in a moment of vulnerability, he confesses, "I'm like Tinkerbell; without applause, I die."[10] Restlessness keeps the pedal to the metal.

To offer a suggestive analogy in this vein: several years ago there was a recall on some Toyota vehicles. Evidently the cars would be given to sudden and uncontrollable acceleration. Terrifying. But as Malcolm Gladwell uncovered in an episode of his podcast

Revisionist History, in most instances people did not even try to use the brake pedal.[11] When the gas pedal malfunctioned, they panicked—and kept pushing the gas. In one tragic instance, the driver of a carload of people kept accelerating until the vehicle went off a cliff.

The upshot of the analogy is clear. Restless ambition, like Conan O'Brien and the Toyota snafu, just can't stop. Inevitably it leads to burnout and worse. As journalist Erin Griffith wrote in an article for *The New York Times*, "For congregants of the Cathedral of Perpetual Hustle, spending time on anything that's non-work related has become a reason to feel guilty."[12] Ultimately, restless ambition attempts to stave off existential anguish with frenzied activity—to generate meaning by means of plugging away. But as Solomon wrote so many years ago, "What has a man from all the toil and striving of heart with which he toils beneath the sun? For all his days are full of sorrow, and his work is a vexation. Even in the night his heart does not rest. This also is vanity" (Eccles 2:22-23). The hum of restlessness might temporarily block out quiet desperation, but it cannot quell it.

So there is also an equal and opposite manifestation of quiet desperation: *resigned* ambition. Resignation is desperate surrender: waving the white flag on life. Already in Thoreau's day, he could say that "desperation is confirmed resignation." The hippie generation of the sixties will think of Timothy Leary's famous mantra, "Turn on, tune in, drop out."[13] In our own times it may be reflected in the burgeoning trend of "quiet quitting." The polling firm Gallup defines quiet quitting as the phenomenon of workers "not going above and beyond at work and just meeting their job description." According to Gallup's recent research, "quiet quitters" make up 50 percent of the workforce, and perhaps more.[14]

Once again, as with hustle culture, there may be something to appreciate, if not admire, about this fledgling movement. At its most mature, quiet quitting rightly recognizes the need to keep a career in proper perspective and to rebuff the harmful effects of workism.[15] While the focus so far seems to be on addressing burnout, the gestures toward personal identity and self-worth hint at the larger ramifications to the conversation. This seems to have some promise for addressing the weaknesses of restless ambition.

But quiet quitting undoubtedly has problems of its own. The media guru Arianna Huffington insists, "Quiet quitting isn't just about quitting on a job, it's a step toward quitting on life."[16] Incidentally, it's often mentioned in the same breath as the so-called Great Resignation: the phrase putatively refers to the (generally positive) movement of workers walking away from dead-end jobs, but I'm hard pressed to hear it without detecting a little irony.

Truth to tell, quiet quitting is only the tip of the iceberg when it comes to rampant resignation. Resigned ambition is detected even more acutely among young men. In his book *Heroic Fraternities* author Anthony Bradley, diagnosing the "self-resigned man," writes, "He just wants to be left alone to do what he wants to do as long as he doesn't hurt anyone. He has resigned from caring. . . . He doesn't want to be bothered. He's content playing videos, smoking weed, and hooking up with a girl or two."[17]

This kind of resignation came home to me in a conversation I had with a young guy that I was playing basketball with not long ago. He shared in passing how none of the males from the graduating class at his small rural school (about twenty guys) went on to college. To be sure, college is not the path for everyone, and later in this book we'll make a case for precisely the kind of trades that don't require a conventional four-year degree. But I was struck that not a single one of these young men went the route of higher education and asked him why. "What's the point?" he said. "We all know we're gonna be stuck back here doin' the same junk." I could almost hear the hope seeping out of his heart.

And I would be remiss not to mention a still more grievous manifestation of resignation in the marked increase over the last decade of so-called deaths of despair: lives lost as a result of suicide, substance abuse, and social isolation. It's the quicksand of quiet desperation at its most lethal.

Restless ambition and resigned ambition: in the final analysis, two sides of the same dreadful coin. Whether by desperate busyness or desperate surrender, hope keeps leaking from the hearts of people; the quicksand-suck continues unabated. Nearly two centuries after Henry David Thoreau went to the woods, the cries of quiet desperation have only grown louder.

But all this talk of desperation, quiet or otherwise, surely doesn't apply to genuine Christians, does it? Old Henry David was, at best, an unconventional believer, and in our time and place the tide of faith has decidedly waned, leaving restlessness and resignation in its wake. Surely those who remain followers of Christ are immune to the threat of quiet desperation, are they not? After all, as Hebrews puts it, "We have . . . a sure and steadfast anchor of the soul, a hope that enters into the inner place behind the curtain" (6:19).

In many respects, I believe that this is most certainly true. For those who trust in Christ, properly speaking there can be no despair. Trials, yes; malaise, surely; doubt, most definitely. But despair is the share of those who have altogether abandoned hope, rather than merely struggled with it. It's the fate of Judas, not Peter.

And yet, if I may shift our metaphor, there exists a variant of the strain of quiet desperation that afflicts Christians in particular, and in fact—precisely since we know that the stakes are so high—may prove even more virulent. In order to diagnose it, we need to turn to one of Jesus' stories that has kept me up at night.

The Longing Hopes That Haunt Us

I am haunted by Jesus' parable of the talents. The parable can be found in Matthew 25:14-30 and Luke 19:11-18, with some variations. What follows is my own composite version.

The story is familiar. A nobleman goes on a journey, and when he does he entrusts his property to a trio of servants: to one he gives five talents, to another two, and to still another he gives one talent. Leaving them with no instructions (save to "engage in business," per Luke's version of the story), the man departs. The first two servants proceed to put their master's gifts to work, each of them earning a 100 percent return. The third servant, however, daunted by the prospect of squandering the trust, opts to stash it away, burying it in the ground.

The nobleman returns from his journey to settle accounts with his three servants. To the first two he offers his unqualified approval: "Well done, good and faithful servant!" To the third, however, he expresses unmitigated disappointment. This servant makes matters worse by trying to explain himself: "I knew that you were a hard man, reaping where you do not sow, and I was afraid, and so I buried the talent." The servant's proclaimed prudence, however, is interpreted by the master as cowardice, bordering on impertinence. So the story concludes with the nobleman's chilling command, "Cast the worthless servant into the outer darkness. In that place there will be weeping and gnashing of teeth."

This is the Gospel of the Lord. *Thanks be to God?*

The ending of the parable would seem to make plain why I'm haunted by it: that I am cowed by the prospect of perdition. And to be sure, it's a terrifying possibility—one that I don't take lightly. That said, I'm a Lutheran. I've had beaten into my head (in the most loving way possible, mind you!) that Jesus died and rose to forgive my sins. Most days I'm more certain that I'm saved by grace through faith than that the boiling point of water is 212 degrees Fahrenheit or that 2 + 2 = 4. Worries about my eternal destiny don't typically keep me awake at night. Maybe they should.

In any case, it's not for thoughts of the afterlife that Jesus' story addles me; it's for thoughts of *this* life. The parable brings to light the deep desire of my heart. In the words of one hymn, "all the longing hopes that haunt me."[18] It exposes what I really want from this life now—and perhaps just as significantly, what I *don't* want.

I remember when the realization sunk in. I'm sitting in the class of one of my favorite professors during my final term as a student in grad school, readying to head out into the world as a pastor. We're talking about vocation, calling—God's purpose for your life. I'd been thinking a lot about it at the time. A popular evangelical preacher had a sermon go viral (as much as they could twenty-five years ago), which he later turned into a popular book. The message was simple: don't waste your life. He contrasted a retiree whiling away his golden years collecting stones on the beach with a dauntless octogenarian who died as a missionary in Africa. It was clear which of the two you should be like.[19]

With this message bouncing around my brain, our class turns to Jesus' parable of the talents. The professor reads through it, puts down his Bible, and is quiet for a moment. Then he says, "What this parable tells us is this: use whatever gifts God has given you to the hilt. Don't ever let up until you make a mark for the kingdom. You've got to make it count."

And suddenly I thought, *That's it. I want to make a mark for the kingdom.* The notion took my breath away, it felt so ambitious. I want my life to mean something, to count. I want (it sounds ridiculous to say it out loud) to *do great things for God*. I want to use my talents faithfully, so that at the conclusion of a life well lived I might hear that glorious commendation, "Well done, good and faithful servant!" *That's* what I want.

I know I'm not the only one.

A little while back I was leading a Bible study with a group of young guys, all at the end of their college years. We got to talking about careers and aspirations. Eventually I just put it on the table: What do you want? There was some throat clearing, looking down at the table. No one wanted to go first. Then John, a thoughtful pastor's kid, raised his hand. He bobbed his head back and forth like a shadow-boxer as he got up the gumption to speak. And then he said, "I know this might sound bad, but I want . . . importance." Soon as he said it, John sat upright and cast embarrassed glances at his peers, but they were nodding their heads in agreement. Coming out of the mouth of this humble kid, I could hardly believe it. But I knew exactly what he meant. It wasn't braggadocio or boasting. He wants to put his talents to use in a meaningful way. We all do.

As a pastor I've been privileged to be privy to many of these conversations. It's after the second cup of coffee or when the dessert is almost gone (pastors eat a lot of meals; you may have noticed from their physiques), when the walk has circled the block the third time or when you're standing in the doorway to go. In those fleeting moments of vulnerability, with hushed voices, we sheepishly admit that we want our lives to be lived—in the words of Robert Frost—"for Heaven and the future's sakes."[20] We don't want to bury our talents; we don't want our days to amount to nothing more than a mound of fear-filled hedged bets. We don't want it all to be a waste.

But herein lies the rub. Desires make you vulnerable; acknowledging what you want opens you up to discouragement if it doesn't come to pass. (Recall the Zone of Frustration.) Even more so when we factor in the transcendent, heavenly horizon upon which our dreams rest. Four decades ago Philip Yancey wrote of this with respect to our relationship with the Lord. "For many people there is a large gap between what they expect from their Christian faith and what they actually experience," he wrote in *Disappointment with God*.[21] And in the words of Solomon, "Hope deferred makes the heart sick" (Prov 13:12).

No sooner do we admit that desire for a meaningful life of faith and we are faced with the ice-cold realization, How can my little labors make any difference whatsoever in the vast sweep of history? The prospect of doing enough to make a mark on God's kingdom seems nigh impossible. It's silly. There are seven billion people in the world—and that's just the number who happen to be walking around at the moment! What hope do I have of leaving an impression on this enormous creation?

Some would say, without apology: none. There's no such hope. In his bestselling book *4,000 Weeks: Time Management for Mortals*, author Oliver Burkeman offers this pointed conclusion: "What you do with your life doesn't matter all that much—and when it comes to how you're using your finite time, the universe absolutely could not care less."[22] Now, Burkeman is not writing out of a Christian worldview. We believe that not a single sparrow is forgotten before God. But even the psalmist grasped the point:

> When I look at your heavens, the work of your fingers,
> the moon and the stars, which you have set in place,
> what is man that you are mindful of him,
> and the son of man that you care for him? (Ps 8:3-4)

In the workaday world of everyday life Burkeman's perspective rings all too true. Given the smallness of our circumstances, it's hard not to feel something like an existential inferiority complex.

Try as we might, like Thoreau, to draw a line in the sand of existence, it can't help but feel futile if you are living in the cosmic equivalent of the Sahara Desert. And worse yet, as Burkeman might also point out, it's quicksand: you are sinking all the time. Maybe, as Christians, we don't quite experience quiet desperation, but nevertheless (riffing off of Yancey) we do know quiet *disappointment*. Make no mistake: it's no less debilitating. Yancey writes:

> No one is immune to the downward spiral of disappointment. It happens to televangelists and to ordinary Christians: first comes disappointment, then a seed of doubt, then a response of anger or betrayal. We begin to question whether God is trustworthy, whether we can really stake our lives on him.[23]

Caught in the quicksand, how can we escape? We need a vision that is as solid as desperation is slippery, and as daily as disappointment all too often tends to be. I've found promise in an easy-to-overlook verse tucked away in a lesser read letter of Saint Paul.

The Quiet Ambition

Paul feared that his work had been a waste. He had ministered at length in the Greco-Roman colony of Thessalonica, but he knew that when he left them their faith was precarious. They were new converts, susceptible to outside influences and vulnerable to the incipient challenges of following Christ. Now he finds himself imprisoned with plenty of time to mull over the state of his Thessalonian friends. Finally he has enough of pacing his prison cell and sends his right-hand man, Timothy, to check on the young church. "When I could bear it no longer, I sent to learn about your faith, for fear that somehow the tempter had tempted you and our labor would be in vain" (1 Thess 3:5).

He needn't have feared. Word of their "faith in God has gone forth everywhere, so that we need not say anything" (1:8). So now he writes, not with anxious uncertainty but with fatherly concern. He exhorts them, in tones reminiscent of the parable of the talents, "walk in a manner worthy of God" (2:12). He knows the uphill climb they face: a tiny church within a vast empire, agitated by afflictions and dealing with the realities of life in this present age still marked by sin and death. He knows that some among the Thessalonians will be wrestling with questions not unlike his own: Is this faith thing for nothing? If people are still dying, then what's the point? Does it all really make a difference?

Thus he also brings glad tidings, lest they "grieve as others do who have no hope" (4:13). He reminds them that, in spite of the present toil that they are enduring, Jesus is risen and will yet return to redeem his creation and make all things new—"and so we will always be with the Lord." So he concludes, "encourage one another with these words" (4:13, 17-18). He doesn't want them to be swallowed up by despair.

Nestled within this encouraging dad talk to the Thessalonians, Paul drops some breadcrumbs on a pathway to peace. If you blink, you miss it. Right before gloriously proclaiming the grounds for hope in the resurrection and the promised return of Christ, he lays out, in a few mundane phrases, how hope can unfold in everyday life. Paul writes: "Make it your ambition to live quietly and to tend your own business and to work with your hands, so that you might walk gracefully toward outsiders and have need of nothing" (1 Thess 4:11-12).

A couple of matters here call for closer scrutiny. First off, Paul says, "Make it your ambition. . . ." Now, ambition is a sticky wicket for committed Christians. Paul knows this as well as anyone. A quick search of his letters and you see that "ambition" follows "selfish" the way that "armpit" follows "smelly"; it's practically redundant. The nineteenth-century novelist George Eliot speaks for many believers when she writes, "I feel that my besetting sin is the one of all others most destroying, as it is the fruitful parent of them all, Ambition, a desire insatiable for the esteem of my fellow creatures."[24] From conniving King Rehoboam to scheming Simon the Sorcerer, biblically speaking ambition is nothing to aspire to.

And then there's this other matter. Paul says, "Make it your ambition *to live quietly*." Biblical commentators have long noted that this is an oxymoron, an apparent contradiction in terms. It's as if he said, "Make it your aim to be aimless," or "make it your plan to be spontaneous."[25] What kind of ambition is quiet living? But this latter point resolves the first. After all, sloth is no virtue in the Scriptures. The soul that is utterly absent of ambition is often singled out for scorn; think of how Solomon relentlessly skewers the one he calls the "sluggard." More to our point, no one aims to bury their talent.

Paul therefore puts forth a paradoxical proposal: what you might call an unambitious ambition—or as I put it, "the quiet ambition." What do I mean by the quiet ambition? Simply stated, it's a way that hope takes shape each day. Because if quiet desperation is the slow seeping of hopefulness amid the mundane stuff of existence—what the character Elaine Benes in *Seinfeld* decried as "the excruciating minutiae of everyday life"[26]—then we need a correspondingly quotidian vision to counteract it. As I describe it, the quiet ambition *is* the unambitious ambition. I'll use the phrases interchangeably.

In 1 Thessalonians 4:11-12, Saint Paul has encapsulated the shape of this everyday hope in these simple postures:

- Live quietly
- Tend your own business

- Work with your hands
- Walk gracefully toward outsiders

To be clear, this isn't some Prayer of Jabez–esque "secret" squirreled away in the attic of holy writ. (If you aren't sure what I'm talking about here, you can be grateful you missed part of early 2000s Christian subculture.) It is rather a neat nutshell of biblical teaching and provides a structure for our argument. As we'll see, it's a summary statement of themes that resound throughout the Scriptures.

The quiet ambition is about finding the largeness in littleness. Or to paraphrase Mother Teresa's famous dictum, it's about doing little labors with large love. It is more a matter of calling than climbing, digging deep than going big. Its role models are Eugene Peterson and Wendell Berry, not Joel Osteen and Steve Jobs. This unambitious ambition is a way of being in the world that weds together conviction with contentment, drive with depth. And it can be an antidote to the threat that Thoreau identified, a way to escape the quicksand of quiet desperation by leading quiet lives of hope.

A Very Little

Not long ago, I reread the parable of the talents in the Gospel of Luke, and a detail caught my attention that somehow I had missed. The nobleman returns to settle accounts, and the first servant comes before his master. He presents his offering, humble though it may be. And the rousing heavenly commendation is followed by this: "Because you have been faithful in a very little, you shall have authority over ten cities" (Lk 19:17).

Catch that? *A very little.* Jesus' message isn't that you need to go out and change the world in order to be reckoned faithful; his message is that genuine faithfulness means wisely stewarding whatever gifts you have—however meager they may seem—in order that, by the influence of the Spirit, you might help move the ratchet of the kingdom one tick forward. And in the eyes of the master, that quiet life of hope, the little labor of love carried out in faith, is very large indeed. David too came to recognize God's regard for the little: "What is man that you are mindful of him, and the son of man that you care for him? *Yet you have made him a little lower than the heavenly beings and crowned him with glory and honor*" (Ps 8:4-5, emphasis added). This is the life-giving message of the quiet ambition.

Before we delve deeper into the shape of the quiet ambition, though, we need to interrogate this desire to "do great things for God." Because it is not benign; it has a shadow side, and by facing up to it we will see more clearly not only how the longing itself can go terribly wrong—even apart from the fallout when it's frustrated—but also how Jesus makes possible a more excellent way.

2

MAKING A NAME

THE GIVEN NAME OF one of the most iconic characters in American literature is virtually forgotten. James Gatz was a North Dakota farm boy of middling prospects. His grand ambitions didn't match up with his modest upbringing. The son of "shiftless and unsuccessful farm people," he longed to rise above his humble roots. And so he did what humans have done, or sought to do, from time immemorial: he made a name for himself. Quite literally.

"I suppose he'd had the name ready for a long time, even then," reports the narrator of the novel that bears his (new) name.

> The truth was that Jay Gatsby of West Egg, Long Island, sprang from his Platonic conception of himself. He was a son of God—a phrase which, if it means anything, means just that—and he must be about his Father's business, the service of a vast, vulgar, and meretricious beauty. So he invented just the sort of Jay Gatsby that a seventeen-year-old boy would be likely to invent, and to this conception he was faithful to the end.[1]

The Great Gatsby tells a story that is distinctly American but universally human. For the impulse to "make a name for yourself" has origins nigh on the beginning of civilization itself. It's the evil twin to the noble desire to do great things for God—a pernicious problem that, left to its own devices, will ruin the best-laid schemes of mice and men. Look no further than the ancient denizens of the land of Shinar.

The Burden of Babel

Life can feel so fragile and fleeting, like a sandcastle built at high tide. When the threat of it all being swiftly swept aside looms large over your existence—and that of everyone you know—how do you respond?

As we've seen, this quandary creates the conditions for quiet desperation. It also forms the dramatic backdrop to the famous story of the Tower of Babel in Genesis 11. The preceding chapter of Genesis details the generations of the sons of Noah. After a long list of names that rarely make Social Security's list of the most popular for babies (Nimrod, anyone?), the chapter concludes, "These are the clans of the sons of Noah, according to their genealogies, in their nations, and from these the nations spread abroad on the earth after the flood" (Gen 10:32). Though its waters abated, the memory of the flood that washed the world clean persisted for generations.

Bear this in mind as we continue to the next section:

> Now the whole earth had one language and the same words. And as people migrated from the east, they found a plain in the land of Shinar and settled there. And they said to one another, "Come, let us make bricks, and burn them thoroughly." And they had brick for stone, and bitumen for mortar. Then they said, "Come, let us build ourselves a city and a tower with its top in the heavens, and let us make a name for ourselves, lest we be dispersed over the face of the whole earth." And the Lord came down to see the city and

> the tower, which the children of man had built. And the LORD said, "Behold, they are one people, and they have all one language, and this is only the beginning of what they will do. And nothing that they propose to do will now be impossible for them. Come, let us go down and there confuse their language, so that they may not understand one another's speech." So the LORD dispersed them from there over the face of all the earth, and they left off building the city. Therefore its name was called Babel, because there the LORD confused the language of all the earth. And from there the LORD dispersed them over the face of all the earth. (Gen 11:1-9)

For the folks who descend on that plain in the land of Shinar, the visceral *our ancestors experienced this firsthand* recollection of the great flood and its effects is evidently alive and well. "After the flood," Saint Augustine writes, "as if striving to fortify themselves against God, as if there could be anything high for God or anything secure for pride, certain proud men built a tower, ostensibly so that they might not be destroyed by a flood if one came later."[2] The idea of life being swept away is no metaphor to them. It's happened before; divine promises and rainbows notwithstanding, they think, it could happen again.

So what do they do? Banding together, as humanity perhaps never had done before and has never done since, they declare, "Come, let us build ourselves a city and a tower with its top in the heavens, and let us make a name for ourselves, lest we be dispersed over the face of the whole earth" (Gen 11:4). Saint John Chrysostom comments, "Notice how the human race, instead of managing to keep to its own boundaries, always longs for more and reaches out for greater things. This is what the human race has lost in particular, not being prepared to recognize the limitations of its own condition but always lusting after more, entertaining ambitions beyond its capacity."[3] And God, having observed the machinations of humankind, promptly comes down to disband the budding building committee and scramble the language of all the earth.

We're most familiar with this story for its connection to human language, and understandably so: it's an arresting feature whose fallout is still felt in innumerable ways. But what interests me here is what it also tells us about human ambition. For the goal of the builders is plain: they wish to "make a name" for themselves, lest they be washed away like a sandcastle—or, indeed, like their ancestors. "They did not desire to hallow God's name," Martin Luther writes, "but they wanted to magnify their own name."[4]

I am convinced that the burden of Babel continues to weigh heavy on human nature in the modern world. We are not so concerned that a flood will deluge our existence, it's true, but still we grapple with the transience and vulnerability of life. Still we wish to put a line in the sand, if not a castle; still we wish to make a name for ourselves.

Only One Hero

Pause for a second to recall that ambition need not be negative. This is illustrated readily enough by the two senses of the Greek word that Paul employs in our theme text from 1 Thessalonians 4. *Philotimeomai* means roughly to be "moved by a love of honor."[5] If this ambition is the selfish love of one's *own* honor (as we see at Babel), then it is plainly negative. If it is for the love of *another's* honor (especially that of the Lord), however, then it can and should be regarded as a good and God-pleasing thing. Indeed, Paul only uses the word positively (see its other uses at Rom 15:20 and 2 Cor 5:9). This distinction makes room for quiet ambition, and it is why biblical scholar Craig Hill writes, "The value of ambition in and of itself is ambiguous. It is the fire that warms the house or, unchecked, burns it to the ground."[6] I mention this because I want to make clear that it is in this latter, house-burning sense of ambition that we best understand the desire to make a name for ourselves.

In her book *Celebrities for Jesus*, author Katelyn Beaty documents in painful detail how horribly this desire can go wrong.[7] Beaty recounts, for example, the story of Bill Hybels, founding pastor of Willow Creek Community Church in suburban Chicago. Hybels possessed a public persona that made him look like the Tom Hanks of ministers—"America's Dad," with classic good looks and endearing charisma. He started out in the 1970s with a desire to realize the Acts 2 vision of the local church, in which believers gather together corporately and in small groups in order to devote themselves "to the apostles' teaching and the fellowship, to the breaking of bread and the prayers" (Acts 2:42). And for a time under his leadership, Willow Creek looked to be doing just that. Meeting in a local movie theater (before that was *de rigueur* for church plants), the congregation grew from around one hundred members to over one thousand in less than three years.

As the congregation grew, however, so too did the platform and acclaim of its pastor. In 1992 Hybels launched the Willow Creek Association in order to spread abroad his ideas about how to lead growing churches. "The Acts 2 vision of church that had launched his ministry career was surely still compelling," Beaty writes. "But running a business for other businesses that wanted to replicate your success proved especially intoxicating." Over time, as he made a name for himself nationally (and even internationally), Hybels became less known by his own congregants. And behind closed doors, a "culture of fear, controlling behavior, and board capitulation" took hold in the congregation. Matters came to a head in early 2018 when Hybels was credibly accused of a pattern of sexual harassment stretching back decades. He resigned from his position in April 2018.

Hybels's story is a cautionary tale of the toxic cocktail of faith and ambition—and it's hardly the only one. Beaty goes on to detail the accounts of other "celebrity Christians," such as Mark Driscoll, Carl Lentz, and Ravi Zacharias, who each achieved spectacular notoriety and experienced stupendous falls. Over and over again, their *hamartia*, their "tragic flaw," is the prideful ambition to make a name for themselves.[8]

We would be wrong, however, merely to shake our heads at the spectacular falls of celebrity Christians, lamenting that they fell prey to the seductions of selfish ambition. The painful truth is that every one of us is complicit in it and susceptible to it. "Celebrities wouldn't exist without us," Beaty warns:

> They depend on our attention and adoration. We look to them to model who we want to become. Being around them makes us feel special and important. We feed their egos, and they feed ours. When a celebrity pastor invites us to join in their mission of changing the world for Jesus, we get excited that we've been selected for greatness. They fulfill what we've wanted to become: really important people for Jesus.[9]

Goals that begin as righteous and good are quickly corrupted when the old Adam sticks his crooked nose into them. The stated intent to "do great things for God" easily elides the all-important last two words. I know that I'm not immune.

When I first took the call to the parish I served in rural northern Michigan, I was feeling pretty good about myself. And frankly, most of the congregants did little to discourage it. The congregation, like so many country churches, had fallen on hard times. Its surrounding community was graying and shrinking, and the dreaded "woe is me" attitude had started to creep in. For a young(ish) preacher with a family—and a doctorate to boot!—to be willing to come and serve . . . why, in their eyes I could nearly walk on water! But then I had a sobering conversation with a brother pastor that I'll never forget.

Josh and I are about the same age, and we were installed as shepherds of our respective congregations only a week apart. Whereas I'm the energetic, get-up-and-go type, Josh is the speak-softly-and-carry-a-big-stick type. He's a bigger guy and with his size carries a certain gravitas about him that belies his age. If not for his Millennial affection for '90s pop culture, I'd swear he was a member of the greatest generation.

One day, early in our respective pastorates, we rode together to a meeting a couple of hours away. On the way back, I subjected him to a succession of humble brags about what dire straits my congregation had been in but how (*aww, shucks*) God was using me to bring it back from the brink. I went on in this vein for some time, and Josh suffered (in the full sense of the term) my blathering. Finally, I gave him leeway in the conversation to speak up—preferably to laud my outstanding efforts. After a moment's quiet, and simply staring out the windshield at the road, he said, "You know, Ryan, pastors don't make good heroes. We've already got a Hero, and it's our job just to point to him." And then he shut up.

Welp: fork, knife, crow.

Though it stung at the time (and still does in retrospect), I am so grateful for Josh's wise counsel. He caused me to reevaluate my early ministry at the church and repent of that all-too-human temptation to make a name for myself. My job wasn't—isn't—to be a hero, but to point to our Hero. I'm no celebrity, but the same strain exists in me that's in Mark Driscoll and Carl Lentz. And it's in you too.

The desire to make a mark for the kingdom, to make your life count, can all too easily devolve into the selfish ambition that seeks personal glory. Making a name for yourself is not the aim of the Christian life. We already have a Hero. And he turns selfish ambition, and the quest to make a name for yourself, upside down.

Downward Mobility

Was Jesus ambitious?

Answering this question can get us a ways toward where we want to go. But it's not nearly so straightforward as it might seem. For as we should have come to expect, the Son of God is not easily cornered.

Let's start with his name. The angel of the Lord tells Joseph in a dream, "You shall call his name Jesus, for he will save his people from their sins" (Mt 1:21). Jesus, Yeshu'a: literally, "YHWH saves." Right out of the gate that's a tall task, to put it mildly. But it's also one that, as he grows up, Jesus doesn't shy away from.

Where to begin? Commonly we'll look to Jesus' "I AM" statements: I am the light of the world, the bread of life, the good shepherd, or simply I AM—the naked assertion of identification with the God of Israel who revealed himself to Moses in the burning bush (Ex 3:14). These statements undoubtedly speak to Jesus' awareness of his divine identity. Less often attended to, but perhaps more pertinent for our purposes, are Jesus' "I came" statements: his expressions of personal mission and aim. Which is to say, his ambition.

"The thief comes only to steal and kill and destroy," he says. "*I came* that they may have life and have it abundantly" (Jn 10:10). He tells the grumbling Pharisees, "*I came* not to call the righteous, but sinners" (Mt 9:13). He says, "*I have come* down from heaven, not to do my own will but the will of him who sent me" (Jn 6:38). And again, laying it out plainly, "I did not come to judge the world but *to save* the world" (Jn 12:47, emphasis mine in the preceding verses). To say that Jesus is ambitious is like saying the universe is pretty big; it understates the case by exponential orders of magnitude. For his aim is nothing less than the restoration of the cosmos: "Behold, I am making all things new" (Rev 21:5).

Given these cosmically grand ambitions, then, how would you expect him to carry them out? Perhaps there would be a celestial message campaign: notes from on high, written in the sky. Or if not composed in the clouds, then at least by means of mass media: a flood of letters, drafted by the Savior and sent to each doorstep—divine direct mail. Or a worldwide speaking tour: a globe-trotting, whistle-stop campaign that would make the indefatigable Teddy Roosevelt look like a puttering homebody. Or at the very least, the establishment of a prominent platform in Rome or Alexandria—some ancient metroplex, from which he could propagate his teaching and catalyze a movement. Any and all of these tactics would befit the grand ambitions of one who claims he came to save the world.

And yet Jesus eschews it all. He wrote nothing, in the sky or otherwise. He came from a town so tiny and backward that it elicited the derisive question from one of his future disciples, "Can anything good come out of Nazareth?" When crowds grew and fame loomed, he retreated to desolate places—or, alternatively, unleashed decidedly unpopular teachings, like, "If anyone doesn't hate his family he can't be my disciple."[10] (Where's the PR team when you need them?) And given the opportunity to shortcut his mission and lay claim to "all the kingdoms of the world and their glory" by simply offering his obeisance to the tempter, Jesus emphatically declines. For someone who supposedly has such exalted aims, he sure has a strange way of pursuing them.

When we zoom out and see the whole heavenly picture, though, ministry backwaters, difficult sermons, and diabolical temptations aren't the half of it. In Philippians 2, Paul paints a picture of downward mobility that takes your breath away:

> [Christ Jesus], though he was in the form of God, did not count equality with God a thing to be grasped, but emptied himself, by taking the form of a servant, being born in the likeness of men. And being found in human form, he humbled himself by becoming obedient to the point of death, even death on a cross. (Phil 2:6-8)

This is almost an exact inversion of Babel. Rather than greedily grasping for security, Jesus generously surrenders divine equality. Instead of scaling the heights of heaven, he willingly descends into the depths. He passes ambitious humanity on the way down the ladder. It makes no earthly sense.

And why does he do it? Jesus bottoms out to lift us up. Out of love for the honor of the Father and his fallen creatures, he dove down into the quicksand of desperation and climbed into the maw of death in order to rescue us from its dread clutches. As the beloved hymn "What Wondrous Love Is This?" puts it, with repetition that can only be called profound,

> When I was sinking down,
> sinking down, sinking down,
> when I was sinking down,
> sinking down—
> when I was sinking down
> beneath God's righteous frown,
> Christ laid aside his crown
> for my soul, for my soul,

> Christ laid aside his crown
> for my soul.[11]

So that we would not sink down eternally, Jesus was willingly swallowed by the quicksand, drowned in the flood.

But then a remarkable thing happens:

> God . . . highly exalted him and bestowed on him the name that is above every name, so that at the name of Jesus every knee should bow, in heaven and on earth and under the earth, and every tongue confess that Jesus Christ is Lord, to the glory of God the Father. (Phil 2:9-11)

God did not leave his Son to languish in the prison house of death. The Father vindicates Jesus' faithful obedience, his downward mobility, by raising him from the dead. As Christ speaks through the voice of the psalmist, "[The LORD] drew me up from the pit of destruction, out of the miry bog, and set my feet upon a rock, making my steps secure" (Ps 40:2). And what is more: Jesus did not seek to make a name himself. Instead, the Father bestowed on him "the name that is above every name." In Christ, the way of the world is utterly upended.

So was Jesus ambitious or unambitious? We have to say that the answer is . . . *yes*. He is the paragon of unambitious ambition.

This makes all the difference as we seek to lead lives that count, that make a mark for the kingdom. We do not need, like James Gatz or the Babelites, to make a name for ourselves. Jesus has made a name for us and bestows it on us. Recall his last word spoken in Matthew's Gospel, the so-called Great Commission: "Go therefore and make disciples of all nations, baptizing them *in the name* of the Father, and of the Son, and of the Holy Spirit" (Mt 28:19-20, emphasis added). When we are baptized, we're given the name of God almighty. We don't need to climb up the ladder to make our lives matter. Jesus climbed down it to ensure that they already do, more than we could ever know.

Not for Nothing

I could've used my tears to conduct the baptism. Luke was a quiet sixteen-year-old when I first met him. But on the day he was baptized, Luke spoke loud and clear so that Grandma Schmidt in the back pew could hear. The skinny teenager renounced the devil's works and ways and professed his faith in the triune God. He was doused from the font, but he might have been daubed from my moist eyes. It had been quite a journey.

Luke's family is like a lot of families in contemporary America. They're blue-collar folks who work with their hands and love their community. His dad, John, works a trade and his mom, Suzie, cares for her aging father and tends their land, selling eggs in a roadside stand to make a few extra bucks. Like many country folks, nothing about their life looked especially remarkable or noteworthy, and they were content to have it that way. But then one day they became front-page news—for the worst reason.

Suzie and John had two boys: Luke and his older brother, Todd. Fun-loving and free-spirited, Todd was the toast of his family, if not the town. He was a big teddy bear of a kid, with a million-dollar smile and an infectious laugh. He starred on the wrestling team and looked forward to working at a local engineering firm. His future was bright and full of potential. Luke adored him.

A year and a half before Luke's baptism, though, Todd graduated high school, and in the ensuing weekend tragedy struck. Saturday, it was all celebration at one graduation party after another. Sunday morning, however, Todd's parents found him in his bed, unresponsive. The news shook the community to its core. No one was shaken more than Luke. His beloved brother, filled with so much promise, was snatched away in an instant.

The family had not been especially religious; to my knowledge none of them had darkened the door of a church in ages. But a year or so after his brother's death, in one of many difficult days for him and the family, Luke was invited to worship by his buddy Ricky, a member of our church. Luke grudgingly agreed at first, but before long he became a mainstay. Not only was he attending worship weekly and participating in youth group, he was even singing in the choir and volunteering to help with potlucks.

One Sunday after he had been around for a few months we had the baptism of a plump little baby named Amos. During coffee hour afterward, with a donut in one hand, Luke nabbed me with the other. "I want to be baptized," he blurted out. "I've never been baptized and I really want to be." He had all the urgency of a six-year-old looking for a potty after drinking a Big Gulp.

"Okay," I said, feeling him out. "But why do you want to be baptized?" As Lutherans, we baptize babies without blinking an eye. When you've got no say in the matter we'll dunk you faster than Lebron with a basketball, trusting in the promises of God.[12] But with someone who is "of age," you might say, we'll take a little more time. After all, teenagers are susceptible to all manner of peer pressure. Maybe Luke had just been getting caught up in the joy of his newfound community. That's not the worst thing in the world, of course, but I wanted to suss out a deeper reason.

I'll never forget what he said next.

Luke was quiet for a moment, and I could almost see Todd's memory flash before his eyes. With a quiver in his voice, he said, "I don't want to feel my life's for nothing. I know Jesus makes it not for nothing. That's why I want to be baptized."

Not for nothing. Hard to argue with that.

So it was that on Easter Sunday, his parents seated in the pews, Luke came forth to enter the kingdom. And as the waters rolled down his forehead and I recited the triune formula, the Lord made a name for him.

In 1 Corinthians 15:58, at the end of his soaring chapter extolling the wonder of Jesus' bodily resurrection—and the promise of our own—Paul concludes on a note that could be called anticlimactic. He writes, "Therefore, my beloved brothers, be steadfast, immovable, always abounding in the work of the Lord, knowing that in the Lord your labor is not in vain." One might think, Where's the final note about eternal life? *When we've been there ten thousand years, bright shining as the sun* and all that. Instead, we're suddenly thrust back into the mundane realm of daily labor?

But this is just the thing. Since Jesus is risen from the dead, our lives—however little they might seem—are caught up into the grand plans of God. Because Christ has given us his name, our daily labor, carried out in faith, has lasting worth. That's the upshot of the resurrection. Our lives are not for nothing.

This is the hope that we cling to and eagerly anticipate. But as Wendell Berry poetically puts it, "Whatever is foreseen in joy / must be lived out from day to day."[13] What I have called the quiet ambition is a way for this hope to take shape in everyday life. It provides steppingstones amid the quicksand of quiet desperation into the "freedom of the glory of the children of God" (Rom 8:21). By leading quiet lives of hope, we can escape the quiet desperation of our age.

Now that we've seen how Christ has "set my feet upon the rock, making my steps secure," it's time to go deeper into the substance of the quiet ambition. Cover your ears: to start with, it's gonna get noisy.

Practicing the Quiet Ambition

The quiet ambition is a way that hope takes shape each day. If our faith can't be lived, if it can't take on flesh and move into the neighborhood, then it remains a pious pipe dream or an abstract idea. "The fear of the Lord is the beginning of wisdom," sings the psalmist, "all those who practice it have a good understanding" (Ps 111:10). Hope takes practice.

In this spirit (and Spirit), each part of this book concludes with some guidance for applying what we are learning to everyday life through practices and spiritual disciplines. Think of these simply as godly habits. They are carried out not in an anxious concern for moral rectitude but from a holy longing to be conformed to Christ more and more, and always with the supplication of the Holy Spirit. "Therefore, as you received Christ Jesus the Lord, so walk in him, rooted and built up in him and established in the faith, just as you were taught, abounding in thanksgiving" (Col 2:6-7).

Suggestions for practicing quiet ambition

1. **Confess your ambitions.** To confess means both to make known and to admit wrong. Let's lean into both those definitions as we start our journey of the quiet ambition by reflecting on our own hopes and desires, and holding them up to the purposes of Christ and his kingdom.

- Pray Psalm 139, which concludes with the petition, "Search me, O God, and know my heart! Try me and know my thoughts! And see if there be any grievous way in me" (vv. 23-24). Ask God to make known the desires of your heart.
- Devote some time to quiet reflection and journaling about what some of your own aims and ambitions are. What do you want? You might revisit Jesus' "I came" statements and draft some of your own. See how yours accord with the Lord's.
- Set a time to meet with your pastor or other spiritual guide for private confession and absolution. Where you recognize that your ambitions have been selfish, repent and confess them—and receive the balm of God's forgiving love.

2. **Remember your baptism.** The triune God placed his name upon you in baptism and claimed you as his own. In my Lutheran tradition, we speak of "remembering your baptism" as a daily habit of recalling who and whose you are. Your value is not defined by your successes (or failures); it is defined by Christ and his work on your behalf. Remembering your baptism, then, is about cementing your identity in Christ.

   - In his Small Catechism, Martin Luther encourages us to bracket our days by making the sign of the cross and speaking over ourselves the name of Father, Son, and Holy Spirit. Practice this habit each morning this week when you wake up and each night before you drift off to sleep. If you are married, consider practicing this with your spouse.
   - Frame a picture or certificate of your baptism on a wall in your bedroom or other place that you'll see it regularly.

- Recite the liturgy "For Those Who Have Not Done Great Things for God" from *Every Moment Holy* with a trusted friend. (If you don't own a copy of the book, this specific liturgy can be downloaded for a small fee at www.every momentholy.com.) Take heart: he is the Lord who enlarges the little!

Part 2

LIVE QUIETLY

3

NOISEMAKERS

THEY'RE JUST WAITING FOR YOU to make a noise.

In the 2018 horror movie *A Quiet Place*, aliens have invaded our world. Fast-moving and fierce, they devour their prey with pitiless dispatch. We follow our heroes, the Abbot family, as they seek to survive in this new postapocalyptic existence. Their family farm is outfitted with ingenious booby traps and security measures.

But there's something different about these monsters: they can't see. Instead, they depend on exquisitely sensitive hearing in order to find and flail their victims. Consequently, noisemakers that might have proved a petty annoyance suddenly become an existential threat. We learn this with heartbreaking clarity when, at the beginning of the film, the Abbot's youngest child mistakenly turns on a noisy battery-operated rocket ship. The monsters were waiting for just such a noise to pounce.

The film is captivating precisely because the strictures of its premise are inconceivable in our contemporary age. As Brian Tallerico wrote in a review for RogerEbert.com, "We live in such a noisy world that it's hard to imagine that constant sound being taken away. We use noise to express ourselves—it's a part of who we are as people. And *A Quiet Place* weaponizes that part of the human condition."[1]

The movie is irresistibly metaphorical. For it is undoubtedly the case that noise can be weaponized by the world, our sinful nature, and the all-too-real monster we know as Satan. We too have "noise-makers" that prove to be existential threats, and as we strive to live quiet lives of hope we need to notice and name them for what they are. This starts with recognizing that "noise" takes on a variety of meanings in our modern world.

Defining Noise

Nate Silver doesn't sense noise the way that most of us do. When you and I think of noise, we think of traffic and train whistles, talking heads and pinging phones. Noise is clamor: the onrush of sounds that clog up our hearing more than any earwax ever could.

Silver and others in his field of research have a more specialized definition. Silver is a statistician. He rose to prominence as a political pollster, accurately predicting the results in forty-nine of fifty states in the 2008 presidential election. In 2009 *Time* magazine called him one of their one hundred most influential people. He has made a successful career of picking up on things that others have missed.

The key to this success has been blocking out noise—but not with fancy headphones. "The world has come a long way since the days of the printing press," he writes. "Information is no longer a scarce commodity; we have more of it than we know what to do with. But relatively little of it is useful. We perceive selectively, subjectively, and without much self-regard for the distortions that this causes." The challenge, then, is to find and focus on the "signal": the meaningful message, the statistically significant data, the stuff that well and truly matters. Thus Silver gives us an elegant definition for *noise*: "The signal is the truth. The noise is what distracts us from the truth."[2]

The noise is what distracts us from the truth. Saint Paul could hardly have put it better. In the terms of our topic here, we might say that noise is the static that distracts us from leading quiet lives of hope. This undoubtedly includes actual, audible clamor and clang. We are hard-pressed to abide in peace when we can't find the first bit of peace and quiet. Consequently, as we'll see, the first noisemakers that we need to address are the sources of loudness in our lives.

Inspired by Silver's broad definition of the term, however, it's easy to see (or hear) how noise permeates our contemporary existence. It's all the stuff that pulls us away from our One Thing. It's the static that keeps us from detecting the divine signal and reflecting the divine Savior. It's what distracts us from the truth of God. Modern life provides no shortage of such noise.

I approach this not like a statistician but like a soul physician. I want to diagnose a few of those noisemakers in our lives that imperil our spiritual health. My prayer is that of Saint Paul, writing to the Philippians: "That your love will overflow more and more, and that you will keep on growing in knowledge and understanding. *For I want you to understand what really matters*" (1:9-10 NLT, emphasis added).

With this definition of noise in mind, then, what are some of the salient noisemakers that threaten us?

Noise All Around Us

The natural place to start with is the actual noise that swirls all around us. Our days echo with din and dings. Most of us have accustomed ourselves to existing with a low-grade hum in the background, like living inside of a refrigerator. If it isn't the demands of bosses then it's the honking of traffic, the buzz of a smartwatch, or a sales pitch on TV.

This is not to say that all of it is bad. There is an eerie quiet that can occupy the houses of some of the homebound widows that I visit. Though I often bristle when my kids are shouting, I wouldn't trade the racket of their calls for all the solitude of Tibet. Suffice it to say, though, we live in noisy times, and it's not all good.

Just ask Gordon Hempton. As an acoustic ecologist and sound recordist (how's that for a cool job?), Hempton has a unique perspective on the state of human-generated noise (as opposed to naturally occurring sound) in contemporary culture. In his book *One Square Inch of Silence* he writes, "Even in wilderness areas and our national parks, the average noise-free interval has shrunk to less than five minutes during daylight hours. By my reckoning, the rate of quiet places extinction vastly exceeds the rate of species extinction. Today there are fewer than a dozen quiet places left in the United States."[3]

When Hempton began his career recording nature sounds in the 1980s, his native state of Washington had twenty-one places that could sustain noise-free intervals of fifteen minutes or longer; three decades later, only three of those places remain. A similar story is told all over the country. He quotes Nobel Prize–winning scientist Robert Koch: "The day will come when man will have to fight noise as inexorably as cholera and the plague." Koch wrote those words in 1905.

In response, Hempton began a quixotic quest for quiet that has culminated in the creation of "one square inch of silence"—literally. Hempton has established a minuscule zone of quiet in Olympic National Park in Washington that is protected (albeit haphazardly) by a policy of the National Park Service. Quiet, he reasons, can ripple out just like noise does.

Hempton's solution is extreme and a little eccentric, but it underscores what we are up against. When my family and I moved to our tiny town in a relatively remote region of Michigan, one of the things we most looked forward to was the fabled peace and quiet of the country. In many respects we were not disappointed: the decibel level is indubitably lower there than in the city, especially when you take hikes deep in the forest.

And yet even in the country there is noise that is inescapable. When we first moved to northern Michigan, I went outside for an early morning walk on a clear, crisp mid-November day. I was soaking up the silent sunrise, when all of a sudden I was cast out of my reverie with the POP POP POP POP! of gunshots. It was all I could do to keep from hitting the deck. Had I suddenly teleported to the mean streets of the inner city? Nope. It was the first day of hunting season. Rural communities, I soon learned, have their own brand of noise, from the engine brakes of semi-trucks on the distant highway to the *brrring* of chainsaws on the neighbor's farm.

The Bible is hardly neutral about noise. Think, for instance, of one of the Lord's most oft-repeated admonitions, going back to the Shema: "Hear, O Israel!" (Deut 6:4). Likewise Jesus' summons: "Let him who has ears to hear, hear." This spiritual hearing surely includes more than simple quiet, but not less than that. As Solomon put it, "Better is a handful of quietness than two hands full of toil and a striving after wind" (Eccles 4:6).

Thus, the first noisemaker that compromises our capacity to lead quiet lives of hope is straightforwardly noise itself. We need to be able to carve out our own "one square inch of silence." But there is plenty of static to distract us in other areas of our lives as well.

Noise in Our Calendars: Busyness

In an interview with journalist Ken Myers for Mars Hill Audio, pastor and author Arthur Boers shared a painfully humorous anecdote. Boers recounted how, in working with the elders of his congregation, they determined several besetting issues for the members of his parish: relationship strain, biblical illiteracy, lax spiritual disciplines. But the one that came up more than any other, and indeed which impinged on all the others, was the issue of busyness. God's people felt too doggone busy, and they were appealing to the spiritual leadership of the church for help.

Boers shared how seriously the elders took this concern, how grave their aspect, how resolved their intention to address it forthwith. But then they set it aside, not to revisit it for two years. Why? Because, Boers explained, the elders themselves were too busy.[4] *Womp womp.*

The story has become all too common in contemporary society. If our calendars could make noise, they would erupt with the interjections of harried travelers squeezing into an overfull subway car. "Hey, watch it!" "I'm in this spot already!" "Move it, there's no room!" It's often pointed out that in the not-too-distant past, when people were asked the anodyne question "How ya doing?" they would too quickly respond "fine" (even when they were not fine). Nowadays, though, the overwhelming (and overwhelmed) answer is, "Busy! Just so, so busy."

Author John Mark Comer tells of a conversation that his friend had with the great spiritual writer and theologian Dallas Willard. The man reportedly asked Willard what was the key to spiritual growth and maturity. Willard, in the true fashion of sages, was silent for a moment. And then he said, "You must ruthlessly eliminate hurry from your life." *Yes, and* . . . the man wondered. "That's it," Willard asserted.[5]

In the quest to lead quiet lives of hope, our cluttered calendars will prove for many of us to be the loudest noisemaker. We're like Mickey Mouse in Disney's rendition of *The Sorcerer's Apprentice,* conjuring more and more supposedly time-saving devices that, weirdly, only seem to multiply our headaches. No sooner is this fire put out then that practice is rescheduled, and "Those meetings are really important, can you please be there?" and *These shows on Netflix sure as heck aren't going to watch themselves!*

There is, to be sure, a measure of this busyness that is not only necessary but positively good. Other people depend on you: your family, your neighbors, your coworkers. You want to work well, thrive in your vocations, be a "good and faithful servant." This is good and right.

But much of the hurried, harried busyness, I am persuaded, stems from the fear of quiet desperation. *If I can stay busy, I won't have to face myself and my problems.* And yet the quicksand doesn't quit.

To paraphrase the title of an old book, we're too busy *not* to quiet the noisemakers. And these noisy calendars are at the top of the list.

Noise in Our Pockets: Devices

Odysseus knew the danger. He had been warned of the Sirens. Their beautiful songs were so powerful that they could distract a sailor from his goal—in Odysseus's case, returning home to Ithaca. What's worse, the Sirens weren't benign figures: their aim was to lure unwitting mariners so that, drawn in by the mellifluous sounds, they would dash their ships against the rocks. So Odysseus took extreme measures. He stuffed the crew's ears with beeswax so that they couldn't hear the songs, and insisted that he himself be lashed to the mast of the ship lest he be lured off course. The hope of home depended upon it.[6]

I take this brief foray into ancient Greek mythology because we have completed almost an exact historical inversion of Odysseus's quest. The Sirens continue their songs unabated. But now, not only do we not resist them at all costs, we put them in our pockets and give them full reign over our lives. Today's Sirens take the form of our devices, smartphones chief among them, and though at times the songs they emit may sound sweet, in the end it's a lot of noise.

We've alluded already to the pings and dings that have become so ever-present. But the actual sounds produced by our phones are only the tip of the noise iceberg. These devices are finely tuned, exquisitely honed distraction machines. If you were trying to introduce as much static into everyday life as possible, you'd be hard pressed to generate something more effective than the Sirens we voluntarily strap to ourselves every day.

Jeremiads against the smart-device-industrial complex have become so commonplace as to be trite, so I don't wish simply to add to the, well, noise. Adults can and should know better by now than to surrender themselves to the alluring effects of smartphones and their ilk.[7] But we ought to attend more closely to what this noise is doing to our kids.

I traveled to a gathering of pastors at a Christian youth camp in north Idaho a couple of years ago. The camp director gave a presentation, and then opened up time for questions. His answer to one question in particular has stayed with me.

One of the pastors asked, "What do kids say is their favorite part about coming to camp?" We're thinking swimming in the lake, time with friends, nonstop flow of sugar from the trading post . . . something along those lines. But the director doesn't hesitate before answering, "There are no cell phones." We all laugh, but he keeps a straight face. "I'm serious. The kids find it a relief not to be always on."

The stats are alarming. Seventy percent of American kids now own a smartphone by age twelve, and more than half by the age of seven—before many of them can even read. On average, they're spending eight hours a day online: a full-time job.[8] And the research of psychologist Jonathan Haidt and others has demonstrated that the precipitous decline in teen and young adult mental health over the last decade can be largely attributed to smartphone and social media usage. "The younger the age of getting the first smartphone," Haidt writes, summarizing a recent study, "the worse the mental health that the young adult reports today." He continues: "There is increasing evidence that smartphones have a variety of detrimental effects on child development including reductions of sleep, focus, and time with friends in person, along with increases in addictive behaviors."[9]

Most poignantly for our purposes, all this noise from our devices also can have profound consequences on the life of faith. Writing in her 2016 book *The Wired Soul*, author Tricia McCary Rhodes lays out some of the spiritual implications of our tech-saturated existence:

- Continually switching from one thing to another trains our brains to seek constant stimulation, making it difficult to spend quiet, focused time with God.
- A steady diet of skimming and scrolling makes us incapable of deep reflection and contemplation, so that we struggle to plumb the depths of God's Word and transcendent truths.
- Compulsive phone use makes us inattentive to people who may be right in front of us: a failure to love our neighbors.[10]

I could go on. When we talk about noisemakers being lethal, these gadgets we find ourselves tethered to are exhibit A. The Siren song threatens to sink the quiet ambition before it even starts.

Noise in Our Hearts: Discontentment

Not all believers number the Ten Commandments the same way. For some Christians (Catholics and Lutherans among them), the prohibition against graven images (Ex 20:4) is subsumed under the first commandment. Then, on the back end, there are two separate commands against coveting: you shall not covet your neighbor's house (ninth), and you shall not covet anything belonging to your neighbor (spouse, animals, and so on; tenth).

Whatever the merits and accuracy of this particular numbering system—and, to be clear, regardless of how they are numbered their content still stands—I've always thought that the doubling up on coveting pointed to a spiritual truth in its own right. To wit: contentment doesn't come naturally. We need two commandments against coveting to underscore how desirous our hearts can be.

And here is where we have to confess that noisemakers do not only come from the outside. It's tempting when thinking of noise to imagine that I am serene in myself—it's the rest of the world that can't keep it down! And you start to sound like a crotchety old neighbor who has his hearing aids turned up too high.

The reality is that the noisemakers that threaten quiet lives of hope emerge not only from without but also from within. And one of those principal interior ones is discontentment. With discontentment, our hearts rattle around inside us like a loose bolt in an engine block. They are restless. In the immortal and oft-quoted words of Saint Augustine's prayer at the beginning of his *Confessions*, "You have made us for yourself, and our hearts are restless until they rest in you."[11]

Psalm 63 is a psalm for the discontented, for those of restless hearts. King David prays, "O God, you are my God; earnestly I seek you; my soul thirsts for you; my flesh faints for you, as in a dry and weary land where there is no water" (v. 1). All that noisome longing in our souls is ultimately clamoring for the Most High, who alone can quiet it.

David continues:

Because your steadfast love is better than life,
  my lips will praise you.
So I will bless you as long as I live;
  in your name I will lift up my hands.
My soul will be satisfied as with fat and rich food,
  and my mouth will praise you with joyful lips. (Psalm 63:3-5)

Discontentment never knows the satisfaction of which David speaks. Whether it's being discontent with the people in your life, the station and vocation God has put you in, the place you find yourself, or the stuff you own, to be chronically discontent is to be constantly distracted from the truth that matters most: Christ is enough. Ironically, discontentment causes you to miss out.

I say ironically because over the last decade or so there's an acronym that has become so pervasive that now it's a punchline: FOMO, the Fear of Missing Out. FOMO is symptomatic of the simmering discontentment promoted by our age and prompted by the panopticon that we call social media. There's always something else you could be doing, someone else you could be seeing, or somewhere else you could be going. Nowadays, the grass is greener not only on the neighbor's lawn but in every facet of existence. FOMO is utterly exhausting and leaves us with the all-too-true words of the Rolling Stones on our lips: "I can't get no satisfaction."[12]

Long before FOMO became a thing (but not before discontentment was), the late, great Rich Mullins wrote a song called "My One Thing." It's an anthem for those who are overwhelmed by the noise of discontentment. He sings, "What will I have when the world is gone if it isn't for the love that goes on and on with my one thing?"[13]

For all the noisemakers that come from without, it's the noise within that may ultimately prove the most damaging. Because only with our one thing—in the words of Martin Luther, "To be God's own and live under Him in His kingdom"—can we sing the song of Mullins and the psalmist rather than the Rolling Stones and our own restive hearts.

Noise in Our Heads: The Evil One

There is one more source of noise that that we would be gravely remiss not to mention, because if it's not behind all the other noise-makers, it's undoubtedly exploiting them like the monsters of *A Quiet Place*. I'm talking about the accusing voice of the evil one, Satan.

People often think of Satan, if they think of him at all, as the temptation guy. He's the one trying to get you to click on that lewd website or say that biting comment to your coworker. This is a well-earned reputation. After all, in perhaps his two most famous appearances—in the Garden with Adam and Eve and in the wilderness with Jesus—his diabolical duty is temptation. Matthew goes so far as to dub him "the tempter."

In reality, tempting is just Satan's side hustle. His real passion, what keeps him going to and fro on the earth, is how he exploits successful temptations: with accusation. Accusing the conscience of humans like a smarmy, ambulance-chasing attorney bringing his case constantly before the bar of heaven. In fact, the very name *Ha-Satan* in Hebrew means "the Accuser."

We see this accusing work in action in a scene captured in the apocalyptic book of Zechariah. As in the more familiar New Testament book of Revelation, Zechariah gives glimpses of what's happening "in the heavenly places." And at one point, we get to see the high priest, named Joshua (not to be confused with Moses' successor), standing in the presence of the Lord. And as he does, Zechariah tells us, "Satan [was] standing at his right hand to accuse him" (Zech 3:1). Of course he was; it's like saying that the baker stood to bake, or the painter to paint. As Saint John will refer to our antagonist in his own vision, he is "the accuser of our brothers," the one who "accuses them day and night before our God" (Rev 12:10).

This noise may be most debilitating of all. It echoes between the ears of the dad who is still beating himself up for not being as present for his kids as they (or he) wished; it knocks around in the heart of the young woman who questions whether she brought that abuse on herself; it resounds in the soul of the pastor who peers out at mostly empty pews and reproaches himself for his apparently fruitless efforts.

More diabolical still, the evil one will happily exploit all-too-real struggles with mental health. The late Michael Gerson spoke to this in a moving sermon delivered at the National Cathedral in 2019.[14] Recounting his own struggles with depression, Gerson describes (in the words of David Brooks) "the lying voices that had taken up residence in his mind, spewing out their vicious clichés: you are a burden to your friends, you have no future, no one would miss you."[15]

Note well: Satan's slithery voice doesn't sound like the cartoon creature on the shoulder. In tones that are all too mundane and even reasonable, his goal is to get in our ears, and in our heads, in order to draw our attention away from God and his truth and instead to ourselves and our failures. Whenever he has done that, and by whatever means, he has succeeded.

To be sure, there is a salutary place for the pangs of conscience. Not for nothing did Adam hide in the garden and fashion his loincloths. His guilt addled his soul. As Saint Paul would write to the Romans, "their conscience also bears witness, and their conflicting thoughts accuse or even excuse them" (Rom 2:15). So for any of us when we violate God's will, the volume of the law written on our hearts suddenly becomes amplified, and rightly so. Like when the music is blared at closing time to tell you that you can't stay any longer, the ache of our hearts is telling us to return home to God.

But this underscores the modus operandi of Satan and how he manipulates sin for his purposes. From the Father's perspective, sin is atoned for. It's finished. He's not wringing his hands over it, at all. Sin thus becomes problematic inasmuch as it drives us away from him. The devil, like he did for Adam and Eve, uses it to drive a wedge between us and our God, who for his part desires nothing more than to be with us.

But how, if sin has been redressed, if "the accuser of our brothers has been thrown down" (Rev 12:10), does Satan still manage to steal our attention and live between our ears (as the kids say) "rent free"? We can't forget that the accuser is also the father of lies (Jn 8:44). And no noise threatens to distract us like the lying voice of the evil one. By his constant assault of accusations, Satan siphons off hope like a hoodlum stealing gas. The result, once again, is quiet desperation, made all the more lethal because we come to believe that our cries are drowned out by the noise of the accuser's recriminations.

Tallying the Impact

"How does one tally the true impact of noise?" asks Gordon Hempton, the audio ecologist we met earlier in this chapter. "You can start with the health effects," he writes: "hearing loss, loss of sleep, possible harm to the unborn fetus, increased risk of heart disease and therefore probably a shortened life span." But he doesn't stop there.

> There are also detrimental effects on learning, decreased productivity, more sick days. Factor in misunderstandings and miscommunication: the wisdom of a teacher or a subtle warming in a first-date dialogue, words uttered but unheard above the din.[16]

Hempton is talking about the costs of the literal loudness all around us, and these ought to be well accounted for. But his inventory also points to a deeper spiritual truth: all this noise is injurious to our relationship with God. All the static distracts us from hearing the voice of our Lord. "My sheep hear my voice," Jesus says, "and I know them, and they follow me" (Jn 10:27). And the prophet Isaiah tells us, "The effect of righteousness will be peace, and the result of righteousness will be quietness and trust forever" (Is 32:17). If we are overcome with loudness, how will we hear his still, small voice?

All the static distracts us from prioritizing what matters most. We flit from one diversion to the next, at varying degrees of importance. We miss the signal straining to break through our crowded calendars. All the static distracts us from living deeply. We succumb to the tyranny of urgency and, to paraphrase C. S. Lewis, flop around in the shallow end of mud puddles—unable to hear the summons to a holiday at the sea.[17]

These noisemakers are not neutral. As we saw with the last one in particular, ultimately they imperil our spiritual lives. Like the monsters of *A Quiet Place*, they lie in wait to weaponize the weaknesses of the human condition. This is why the first part of the quiet ambition is so necessary, and so welcome. In these noisy times, our Lord invites us to "live quietly." What does that look like? To see, we turn to our next chapter.

4

QUIET SAINTS

WHEN THE APOSTLE PAUL encouraged the Thessalonians to "live quietly" it was a message that would have resonated with many in the ancient Greco-Roman world. Abraham Malherbe notes that the Greek word *hesychazein* (it's as easy to pronounce as it looks), which literally means to "be quiet," had "long described withdrawal from active participation in political and social affairs."[1]

The famous Stoic Seneca, for instance, viewed living quietly as a salutary substitute for the frenzied life of public officials; instead, one ought to "meditate and engage in more noble activities."[2] But Malherbe observes, "Sometimes a principled desire to retire from the demands of society to pursue a higher spiritual good is difficult to distinguish from a romanticization of the countryside."[3] Biblically speaking, however, living quietly isn't a romantic ideal; it's a gift of grace. It flows from a heart that is at peace with the Lord and can be lived out most anywhere.

We hear of this throughout the Scriptures. It first appears in dramatic fashion at the shores of the Red Sea. The Israelites have been hunted down by Pharaoh's army and now are grumbling that God ought to have left them in slavery: "It would have been better for us to serve the Egyptians than to die in the desert!" (Ex 14:12). But Moses gives the emphatic reply: "The LORD will fight for you, and you have only to be silent" (Ex 14:14). Quietness signals confidence in God to save.

The prophets also pick up on this theme. For instance, the Lord says through the prophet Isaiah, "In repentance and rest is your salvation, in quietness and trust is your strength" (Is 30:15 NIV; the next phrase, however, is instructive: "but you would have none of it." Noisemakers aren't so easily silenced.) And Zephaniah speaks movingly of this when he says, "The LORD your God is in your midst, a mighty one who will save; he will rejoice over you with gladness; he will quiet you with his love" (Zeph 3:17). The love of the Lord alone can still our restless souls.

The Psalms poetically and prayerfully capture this posture like nothing else can. "For God alone my soul waits in silence," David prays. "From him comes my salvation" (Ps 62:1). And once more, in the famous verse of Psalm 46:10: "Be still, and know that I am God." Living quietly, above all, means leaning on the Lord.

It's with this cultural and biblical background that Saint Paul will then tell us that living quietly is an aim worth praying for: "First of all, then, I urge that supplications, prayers, intercessions, and thanksgivings be made for all people, for kings and all who are in high positions, that we may lead a peaceful and quiet life, godly and dignified in every way. This is good, and it is pleasing in the sight of God our Savior" (1 Tim 2:1-3). God approves of the quiet life.

Which brings us back around, then, to our theme verse of the unambitious ambition: "Make it your ambition to live quietly." The ancients commended it; the Scriptures, while modifying the vision, extolled it. But what does it look like to live quietly? I suspect that for many of us, though we might not be able to name Five Steps to a Quiet Life (which in any case seems contrary to it), we can recognize those people who are doing it, who in some respects embody, if you will, a "godly quietude." They're likely not monks, but rather folks who have a quality of spirit and clarity of vision such that their very lives, to paraphrase the famous line about Teddy Roosevelt, speak softly and carry a big stick.

Over the last few years, as the notion of quiet ambition has stuck with me, I've begun to notice and collect stories of quiet exemplars: people of faith who demonstrate the characteristics of living quietly. In this chapter I want to share a few such sketches. This is by no means a checklist, but as we go I'll lift up some lessons that we can all take from these lives of godly quietude.

Barry Sanders: Quiet Humility

On July 27, 1999, the worst nightmare of my teenage self came to pass. No, I didn't get pantsed in a school assembly or fail my driving test. My dog didn't die, nor did my girlfriend dump me. (I didn't have a girlfriend—although that actually would have been a lot closer to what I did experience.)

Rather, on that lazy summer afternoon, Barry Sanders—my sports idol, my hero, the inimitable running back for the Detroit Lions, the guy that I'd been watching since I was six, whose posters plastered my walls—on that day, Barry summarily called it quits.

You might be thinking, so what? Every pro athlete retires at some point. But Barry was only thirty-one. He was at the pinnacle of his powers. What's more, he was within shouting distance of setting the all-time rushing record in the NFL; one more season and he'd likely do it. And then, just like that, he hung it up. Walked away from it all.

A decade earlier, as Sanders's elusive (in more ways than one) career was just beginning, the famed Detroit journalist Mitch Albom asked, "Who is this guy? What makes him tick?" From the start it was clear that Barry was different. Albom wrote: "Why is that important? Sanders wonders. Isn't it enough that I run? Don't they know what I know? A humble man can do anything without a lot of noise."[4]

Sanders was one of eleven kids, raised in a devout Christian home in Wichita, Kansas. His parents modeled for him a way of living quietly. "They are get-up early, hard-working, go-do-your-job people," he reflected many years after leaving the house. "They don't want anything from anybody. They want to take care of their own. That was exactly my approach to football. I wasn't necessarily looking for fame and fortune. I tried to make sure I upheld my end. I took care of business and then went home."[5]

In an age of self-involved celebrity athletes, no one knew what to make of Barry. "Football is not the most important thing in my life," he said. "Religion, my family, being at peace with myself—and then maybe football."[6]

From the time he was young, Barry thought he might be a preacher. "Most of my life has revolved around Sundays," he quips in his autobiography *Bye Bye Barry*.[7] Long before it was spent on the field, it was in the pew. At home as a six- or seven-year-old, he'd conduct pretend services in the living room, subjecting his siblings to sermons delivered from the La-Z-Boy.

As it happens, his future was not in the pulpit but on the gridiron. But his faith followed him in a way that no defender ever could. When he signed his first contract, complete with a $2.1 million signing bonus, he dumbfounded reporters who caught wind of the fact that he promptly gave a tenth of it to his small Baptist church back in Kansas. "Tithing, it's in the Bible," he explained.

I recall how, especially in his early years, his autographs would always be accompanied by a Scripture verse. "He is for real," Albom observed. "Give him a roof, a bed, some food, and a Bible, and he will want for nothing."[8]

But after a decade of domination on the football field (individually, at least; his Lions' teams were consistently mediocre), Sanders unceremoniously walked away. He didn't even so much as hold an emotional press conference, simply faxed a letter to the team and local news outlets. No muss, no fuss.

For a quarter century, football fans have wondered, why? A recent documentary based on the aforementioned autobiography explores the question at length.[9] It highlights different factors: pressure from his father, the trauma of seeing a pair of teammates separately suffer debilitating neck injuries, his team's poor performance. But ultimately, as longtime sports broadcaster Dan Patrick observes in the film, it was simple. He went out the same way that he came in and the way he went about his business: humbly and quietly.

I think part of why Barry's retirement was so impactful to me is that he truly had been more than a sports figure; he was a role model. Though I didn't have the language for it at the time, he showed me what it looked like to live quietly. It didn't require that he neglect his talent or elect to be a ball boy on the sidelines rather than a running back on the field. Living quietly was rather about how he handled himself, even when he happened upon celebrity. "Go about your work and give glory to God," Barry's mom, Shirley, had taught him. In this way he was teaching me and countless other kids as he simply handed the football to the official after every touchdown, deflected praise to his teammates, and declined to pursue individual accolades.

Barry's vocation was rare, but it's his approach to it that was truly exceptional. But boy it would've been nice to see him break that rushing record. Lions' fans take whatever they can get.

Concerning Hobbits: Quiet Delight

If you were trying to imagine fictional characters that embody this unambitious ambition, you would be hard pressed to do better than the furry-footed, second-breakfast-eating residents of Middle-Earth called hobbits. "Hobbits are an unobtrusive but very ancient people," we are told at the outset of *The Fellowship of the Ring*, "more numerous formerly than they are today; for they love peace and quiet and good tilled earth: a well-ordered and well-farmed countryside was their favorite haunt."[10]

Their creator, J. R. R. Tolkien, was a devout Christian who seemed to have an intuitive grasp of the quiet ambition—in both his life and his writing. In many respects his hobbits exemplify the characteristics that we are talking about in this book, but especially in this respect: "It is clear that Hobbits had lived quietly in Middle-Earth for many long years before other folk became even aware of them."[11] And the quiet lives they lead are particularly apparent in two ways: how they relish the good gifts of creation and how they cherish their home.

Hobbits are not hedonists; they do not pursue pleasure heedlessly. But neither are they Puritans, which has scandalized not a few Christian readers over the years. As author Christopher Snyder points out in his book *Hobbit Virtues*, the hobbits are by no means teetotalers; they enjoy imbibing their beer and smoking their pipes.[12] So what we see in the hobbits is what philosopher Josef Pieper called the spirit of festivity: a joyous affirmation of existence.[13]

This passage from the prologue of the *Lord of the Rings* trilogy captures the spirit well:

> Their faces were as a rule good-natured rather than beautiful, broad, bright-eyed, red-cheeked, with mouths apt to laughter, and to eating and drinking. And laugh they did, and eat, and drink, often and heartily, being fond of simple jests at all times, and of six meals a day (when they could get them). They were hospitable and delighted in parties, and in presents, which they gave away freely and eagerly accepted.[14]

One might argue that six meals a day does indeed sound like hedonism, but one can only imagine the metabolism such busy-bodied little creatures have. In any case, the picture that we get of hobbits is one of delight. They enjoy the good gifts that come their way, whether it be of the earth and its produce, or of people and their company.

Living quietly, you see, does not mean living sparingly. To be sure, simplicity is essential; it is not only a virtue but also a spiritual discipline that accords well with leading quiet lives of hope. But that's different from joyless abstention.

The hobbit habit of relishing good gifts—especially food and drink—is much nearer to how the Orthodox theologian Alexander Schmemann described eating:

> Centuries of secularism have failed to transform eating into something strictly utilitarian. Food is still treated with reverence. A meal is still a rite—the last "natural sacrament" of family and friendship, of life that is more than "eating" and "drinking." People may not understand what that "something more" is, but they nonetheless desire to celebrate it. They are still hungry and thirsty for sacramental life.[15]

To live quietly, then, is to live *eucharistically*: filled with thanksgiving, from the Lord's Table to the supper table.

The other aspect of the hobbit way of living quietly is how they cherish home. Hobbits are not nomads. They are fiercely loyal to their country; they're patriots, in the best sense of the term. To paraphrase Wendell Berry, what they stand for is what they stand on.[16]

This is evidenced, first, in the hesitancy of Bilbo and later Frodo and Sam ever to leave the Shire. It takes a compelling quest to drive them out, "the furthest from home [they] have ever been." It only becomes fully apparent, though, with the full arc of the narrative, culminating with a scene that was left out of the movies: the scouring of the Shire, when the hobbits return and reclaim their home.[17]

The hobbits show us that the quiet life is the rooted life. In his book *Them* (which is more about building strong communities than it is a tract about political division), former senator Ben Sasse writes eloquently of the need for all people—but I would say especially Christians—to commit to a community. He writes,

> When we look for reasons to avoid investing our time or energy or resources in a particular place or at a particular moment, what we're really doing is trying to dodge the call that it might make on us. We're trying to avoid the hard work of digging in. . . . The only community that exists is this one, here and now. But we have to choose to embrace it.[18]

Even when the hobbits Frodo and Sam answered the call to abolish the ring, traveling far from home in the process, it was because of their devotion to their community. That's what cherishing home will do to you.

And so Sasse makes a rather counterintuitive recommendation: buy a cemetery plot. Nothing spells commitment to a place like making it your body's last stop en route to the resurrection. "Buy the cemetery plot, and live in this place," he commends.

> Sure, the people around you are annoying, but the people in the next, "better" place are annoying, too. People everywhere are annoying. Community is hard. So what? Commit anyway, and act as if your body is going to end up in the place where you are. Eventually, you'll be right.[19]

This is not to say that everyone can—or even should—become multigenerational settlers. The needs of work force people to transfer. Family circumstances require relocations. Sasse himself, compelled by his convictions, left the Senate and his native Nebraska in order to become president of the University of Florida. Furthermore, wherever we live we are strangers and exiles in this present age, awaiting "the city that has foundations, whose designer and builder is God" (Heb 11:10).

But because the rooted life flows from our roots in Christ, wherever we happen to dwell we can commit to the community and "seek the welfare of the city where I have sent you into exile" (Jer 29:7). Until finally, when Jesus returns and ushers in the new creation, we can say with satisfaction, as that consummate hobbit Samwise Gamgee did with the final words of *The Lord of the Rings*, "Well, I'm back!"

Rosa Parks: Quiet Strength

Martin Luther King Jr. is rightly remembered as the booming voice of the civil rights movement. His soaring oratory articulated a vision of equality and inspired a nation. But if King's baritone provided the resounding soundtrack of the movement, Parks was its still, small voice. Before King shared his dream in the hearing of a million souls on the Washington Mall, Rosa catalyzed the movement with a single word in the hearing of one white man: "No."

It's December 1, 1955. Forty-two-year-old Rosa has already experienced a lifetime of discrimination. Born and raised in Alabama, she has been denied voting rights, forced off of public transportation, humiliated in front of family and friends. Her faith in Christ and the fellowship of believers inured her to the taunts she daily endured as a girl. "My strength has always come from the church," she writes in her aptly titled autobiography *Quiet Strength*. "I have always gained strength from thinking about the Bible and from the faith of my family. Church has always been a place where we can turn to God for rest and encouragement."[20]

She had chosen instead to follow her Lord and quietly protest the injustice that encompassed her. "I refused to go along with the unfair rules," she wrote. "Back in the segregation days, when I went downtown, I walked up and down the stairs rather than ride elevators marked 'colored.' Often I walked a mile from home to work and then back again rather than ride the bus, because the buses were the worst of the options. On hot days when my throat was dry, I walked past the water fountains marked 'colored' and waited until I got wherever I was going to get something to drink."[21]

So on that fateful day in December 1955, Rosa simply continued a long-established pattern of living quietly. When Parks refused to surrender her seat to a white passenger on board a Montgomery bus, she didn't intend to set into motion the chain of events that would ultimately transform the country. She writes, "When I refused to give up my seat, I had no idea what it would spark or what change would result. I simply did it because I thought nobody else would do anything."[22] It was just the right thing to do.

And transform the country it did. Inspired by (in the words of biographer Gregory J. Reed) her "quiet, courageous act," a flotilla of similar humble protests soon followed: sit-ins, eat-ins, swim-ins . . . you name it. And after 381 days, the Montgomery Bus Boycott prevailed: the US Supreme Court declared bus segregation unconstitutional.

"I had always imagined Rosa Parks as a stately woman with a bold temperament, someone who could easily stand up to a busload of glowering passengers," writes Susan Cain in her 2012 bestseller about the power of introverts, *Quiet*. "But when she died in 2005 at the age of ninety-two, the flood of obituaries recalled her as soft-spoken, sweet, and small in stature. They said she was 'timid and shy,' but had the 'courage of a lion.' They were full of phrases like 'radical humility' and 'quiet fortitude.' . . . Why shouldn't quiet be strong? And what else can quiet do that we don't give it credit for?"[23]

Rosa took "speak softly and carry a big stick" to a new level. A petite, mild-mannered lady who would barely even be a threat to swat a fly, Rosa Parks is nevertheless proof that living quietly doesn't equal quietism—disengagement from the world. What's more, her example shows how this way of life can be a posture of hope in the face of evil and injustice.

I'm reminded of a petition in the great nineteenth-century hymn "God of Grace and God of Glory":

Save us from weak resignation
To the evils we deplore;
Let the gift of Your salvation
Be our glory evermore.[24]

Living quietly does not mean merely going along to get along. To the contrary, as Rosa Parks so ably demonstrated, quiet ambition is an antidote to "weak resignation."

Rich Mullins: Quiet Simplicity

A few weeks after Rich Mullins died in a car accident in 1997 at age forty-one, his friend and financial manager, Jim Dunning, went to collect Rich's possessions. Mullins was a wildly successful Christian musician famous for the songs "Awesome God," "Step by Step," and many other hits. His popularity could have afforded him a luxurious lifestyle. But when Dunning retrieved Rich's things, they didn't fill up half of a twenty-foot moving truck.

"I have clients who made less than Rich, who have seven-thousand-square-foot homes filled with possessions," Dunning recounts in James Bryan Smith's biography, *An Arrow Pointing to*

Heaven. "And here was this guy who, in his entire life, could fill up only eighty square feet."[25]

Rich Mullins, whose song "My One Thing" I quoted in chapter three, exemplified how living quietly goes hand in hand with living simply. Raised on a farm in rural Indiana by a family of Quakers, simplicity was in his blood. James Bryan Smith writes, "Because he lived simply, Rich was free, and many envied this in him. Rich had discovered that when ambition lifts, freedom falls like rain."[26] The unambitious ambition came to him naturally.

Rich never desired to be rich and famous, only to use his gifts to glorify God and lift up his people. He had moved to Nashville, the epicenter of the contemporary Christian music industry, but when he started to become popular, he moved away to Wichita (not exactly known as a musical hotbed). And as his income grew, Rich told Dunning that he didn't want to know how much he actually made, but just be given a salary that corresponded to the average working man's wage—at that time, about $24,000 a year. (Mullins desired to give away the rest.) Dunning reports that when Rich died he had only been spending about two-thirds of even that meager amount.

Rich's sister Debbie tells of a time that she accompanied him to New York City when he had the opportunity to give a concert at the famed Radio City Music Hall—an incredible honor for any musician. After the concert, as the two of them stood on the sidewalk, a stretch limo that had been ordered by the concert organizers pulled up to give them a ride to the hotel. Rich thanked the driver but waived him on, reporting that they'd be riding with his crew in the equipment van. Some time later, a friend asked Debbie, "Do you ever get tired of all these people treating your brother like he is any different from you or anyone else?" And Debbie said, "No, because he *is* different. I would have gotten into the limo!"[27]

In his late thirties at the height of his popularity, Rich went back to school to get a degree in music education. He aspired to teach music and the gospel to Native American kids. His last few years were spent in relative anonymity, serving among the Navajo on a reservation in New Mexico. He had never been happier.

In an article for *Release* magazine titled "Telling the Joke," Rich reflected on how faith did not become real to him due to fine-sounding arguments. "I am a Christian, not because someone explained the nuts and bolts of Christianity to me," he wrote, "but because there were people who were willing to be nuts and bolts."[28] Such people embody the divine comedy—the "joke"—of the gospel. And so he encourages his readers, then and now:

> Live out your lives and, by your living, tell the joke that I, in my writing, so feebly attempt to explain. Love one another, forgive one another, work as unto God, let the peace of Christ reign in your hearts. Make it your ambition to lead quiet lives. No one will argue with that.[29]

The testimony of Rich Mullins's life managed to convey that comedy more than he ever realized.

Saint Helen: Quiet Gratitude

Helen had every reason to be bitter. They say that some people are dealt a bad hand in life, and Helen couldn't muster a pair of twos. She had it hard, and for a long time.

Helen was a member of my congregation. She came into the world amid the Spanish flu epidemic, born in 1919, and lost a sibling before she could speak. Her father died in the shadow of the Great Depression, leaving Helen and her mother alone. "It's just you and me now, sis," Helen recounted her mom saying after the funeral as they walked down the street in Milwaukee, bereft. "We don't have two nickels to rub together." But no sooner had Mom said that then young Helen looked down and saw a shiny new nickel resting innocently on the ground. "Look mom!" Helen exclaimed. "Now we do!"

She married young and became a widow young. Ever a can-do gal, Helen found ways to make a living and keep herself and her two children afloat. She started a printing business. Though it wasn't a moneymaker, she'd print little prayer cards with that iconic painting of Jesus on one side—the head shot in which he has brown, flowing locks and is looking off in the distance[30]—and on the other a simple cry of faith: "You can get me through today, Lord!"

Helen remarried, only to become a widow for the second time before sixty. She lost a daughter, too, well before her time. Life kept dealing her body blows. But that's when Helen got the idea of starting a support group for widows. Her pastor at the time gave her his blessing to host it at church, and the group blossomed into a haven of healing for dozens of women. At the center of it all was the slight, twice-widowed woman who just couldn't stop smiling and pointing people to Jesus.

By the time I met her, Helen was pushing the century mark. She lived alone in a tired old mobile home, plastic flowers "planted" out front and porch lights flickering endlessly like a horror film. It was the world headquarters for an ongoing ministry of listening, care, and prayer. Helen still fielded phone calls from all over the country. People who came over supposedly to help her, like the cleaning lady who visited twice a week, would invariably leave as the beneficiaries of more aid than they gave.

Helen's one hundredth birthday party filled the fellowship hall at church. Sometimes the birthdays for older folks can be a melancholy affair; so many friends have passed on that there are more empty seats than occupied ones. But Helen was a perpetual friend-generation machine. Thus there were folks from all walks of life—the young girl that she encouraged in drama, the Meals on Wheels volunteers, the director of the Council on Aging—whose lives had been touched by the woman I have come to think of as "Saint Helen." She regaled us with tales from the past century and how she had seen things change. ("From a carriage on the road to a computer in your pocket!") But then she was sure to remind us all what hadn't changed, singing a stanza from one of her favorite hymns:

> Great is Thy faithfulness, O God my Father!
> There is no shadow of turning with Thee!
> All I have needed Thy hand hath provided.
> Great is Thy faithfulness, Lord, unto me.[31]

And then we stuffed ourselves with what looked like a wedding cake . . . at Helen's request, of course.

Every time I visited her, Helen had the same anguished plea. At the conclusion of an hour or more spent talking, reading Scripture, celebrating the Lord's Supper, and praying, Helen would reach out her frail hand and grab hold of me. With tears streaming down her face and a smile that glowed, she would ask, "Who could help me count all these blessings? How will I ever number all these gifts from God?"

During her 101st year, she died like she was born: at home, in the midst of a global pandemic. Her life was poetry in more ways than one.

Hope abounded in Helen's life, buoyed by thanksgiving. She lived quietly as she lived gratefully—even (especially) when circumstances didn't seem to warrant it. And to be sure, Helen wasn't Pollyanna; she could be incensed by the world, the devil, and her own sinful flesh as much as the next guy or gal. But in the midst of it all, still she saw nickels from heaven.

There's no color-by-number when it comes to living quietly, but you know it when you see it. I've given you just a sample of some of the saints I've seen leading quiet lives of hope. Who are the ones that have crossed your path? Since they don't make a fuss, they are easy to miss. Maybe we need to pay closer attention.

The Practice of Living Quietly

We live in a restless, noisy age, fraught with myriad noisemakers, from digital technology to traffic to the wiles of the devil. All that noise threatens to distract us from the truth of Christ and his word. "For God alone my soul waits in silence," prays the psalmist, "from him comes my salvation" (Ps 62:1). We endeavor to follow in the footsteps of the countless "quiet saints." What are some steps in that direction?

Suggestions for practicing the quiet ambition

1. **Carve out your own "one square inch of silence."** Finding solitude and silence is a spiritual necessity in our noisy age. Follow Gordon Hempel's example and stake out that space in your schedule. A few ideas:

   - Make your commute a time of quiet for prayerful communion with God, or listen to "psalms, hymns, and spiritual songs" that lift your heart in praise (perhaps one of those in the morning and one in the afternoon).
   - Enjoy a walk without headphones at the end of the workday or over lunch.
   - Schedule an annual all-day retreat for rest, study, and prayerful planning for the months ahead. This can be a challenge if you have a family; set aside the time in advance

and arrange additional childcare if necessary. It's worth the investment.

2. **Think and grow like Rich.** Rich Mullins exemplified the classic discipline of simplicity. You and I may not be able to limit our possessions to less than eighty square feet, especially if (unlike Rich) you have a family. We can, however, aspire to live well below our means, freeing us to give generously and be unencumbered by needless debt. Can you strive to live on closer to two-thirds of your income as Rich did?
3. **Underschedule.** What if we applied the same principle of living below our means to our calendars? Too often we fill our schedules to the brim, like kids with a cup of hot cocoa, and grow harried and anxious when responsibilities and engagements start to spill over. We need more margin.
   - One rule of thumb that I strive for in my family is not to schedule more than three evening outings in a week—whether that be sports, meetings, or gatherings with friends.
   - I have found the fifty-percent-buffer rule to be exceptionally helpful: however long you think a task will take, add fifty percent. For instance, if you expect a meeting to last an hour, budget ninety minutes. If it ends up only being an hour or so, it's like you got a time rebate. Bonus!
4. **Embrace "dumber" phones.** Instead of lashing ourselves to the mast as Odysseus did, we have strapped ourselves to the Sirens. Our phones too often keep us distracted and on edge. We can push back.
   - If your life circumstances require you to have a smartphone, strip it of its most addictive features, especially social media and email apps.

- For a next step, consider adding a Light Phone or the like, which can port the number of your smartphone. Leave the latter at home as often as you can, especially when you are out with family.
- When you are ready to get more radical, trade the smartphone for a "dumb phone" altogether. Your spiritual health—and sanity!—are worth the cost of any inconveniences.

5. **Buy a cemetery plot.** Nothing says *rooted* like reserving the resting place for your earthly remains. Even if your vocation or other circumstances precludes you from staying in one location, choose a place that is close to your heart and purchase cemetery plots nearby (childhood home, summering spot, etc.). We can't all practice the Benedictine vow of stability, but we can seek to root ourselves more deeply to a place and community.

Part 3

TEND YOUR OWN BUSINESS

5

THE BLASPHEMOUS ANXIETY

"JUST WHAT DO YOU THINK YOU'RE DOING?" she said. That's when we froze in our tracks.

Our family was visiting a beloved cherry-themed specialty shop in northern Michigan (an area known as the cherry capital of the world). The shop is famous for its generous samples: big bowls of chocolate-covered cherries, cherry-infused jam, cherry sours, and more have ladles beside them with cups or plates for snacking. It's like the Platonic ideal of freebies: it's not uncommon for families to go out to dinner and then hit up this shop afterward rather than get dessert. Costco, eat your heart out.

On this particular day we were just browsing and, yes, availing ourselves of generous samples. We'd done this probably a dozen times before. But on this occasion, mouth full of white chocolate–covered cherries (my personal favorite) and sizing up cherry cheese, a middle-aged woman who looked like she stepped out of central casting for "school marm" sidled up beside us and made the throat-clearing noise that is the international sign for *Ex-cuse me.*

"Just what do you think you're doing?" she said, as my wife slipped a last few sour cherry gummies into her pocket. "This is not a lunch counter!"

Chastened, the family put our heads down and prepared for the walk of shame out of the shop, our profiles no doubt being snapped by the CCTV and readied for hanging on the wall with the caption, "DO NOT ALLOW THESE FREELOADERS ANYWHERE NEAR THE CHERRY CHUTNEY." But my wife, bless her contrarian soul, was not so quick to hang her head. She said, "I'm sorry, we've just thought . . ."

"You thought WRONG!" the woman exclaimed. People were starting to stare.

But then Anne sized up our prosecutor, and her look changed from humble accommodation to steely resolve. I tugged on her shirt and said, "C'mon, hon, let's go," not wanting to belabor the embarrassment. Yet Anne had noticed that the lady lacked any of the distinguishing accoutrements of other clerks: no screened T-shirt, no apron, no name tag.

"Now, hold on," Anne said with defiance. "Do you even work here?" Folks who had been pretending not to pay attention to the kerfuffle suddenly glanced up.

"Well . . . *no*," the lady said with reluctance. Then, stomping off: "But you shouldn't do that!" I glanced over at the shop counter, where the actual employees were busily checking out (ahem) *paying* customers, and one of them shrugged her shoulders and, with a sympathetic look on her face, mouthed "*I'm sorry*." I nodded my head in acceptance and made my way for the cherry chutney.

In recent years, a name has been pejoratively attached to people like our cherry shop school marm: Karen. A Karen is a rule-following scold who can't keep their nose out of other people's business. The gendered name notwithstanding, a Karen can be a man or woman, young or old. Such people can be found in every sector of society (though they may be disproportionately present on social media). What they hold in common is a predilection for pronouncing, "Well, you shouldn't do that!"

Biblically speaking, though, another name is a byword for such behavior: Martha. And her story keys us in to the more profound spiritual perils of failing to heed what is the second part of the quiet ambition: "tend your own business."

The Preacher's Landmine

There is no shortage of passages in Scripture that give preachers fits. God "changing his mind" about humanity in Genesis 6 is one; Jesus saying of Judas that it'd have been better for him not to have been born is another. There are plenty, and we frankly do our best to skirt them as we are able and handle them gently when we are not. But one passage that truly leaves the preacher shaking in his robe is the story of Mary and Martha in Luke 10.

Oh, on the surface it seems very homely and endearing: Jesus paying a house call on a couple of hospitable sisters. But make no mistake, underneath that veneer is a homiletical minefield. For every congregation is composed of countless "Karens" and myriad "Marthas"—as well as, if you will, "Kevins" and "Marks"—with crossed arms, narrow eyes, and pursed lips, just waiting to put in their resignation from the altar guild or the board of trustees if the preacher takes one false step.

But I get ahead of myself. As the story goes, Jesus and the disciples are passing through the village of Bethany, a couple of miles outside Jerusalem. There, we're told, this woman Martha opened her home to him. Whether she extended this invitation to the Lord or he invited himself is unclear, but if the later account of Zacchaeus is any indication, Jesus was by no means above turning up unexpectedly like Cousin Eddie in *Christmas Vacation*.

I can only imagine Martha's reaction to Jesus' arrival. "Jesus! How good of you to stop by . . . You'd like to come in? Of course, of course. [Side-eyeing Mary to hop to it in the kitchen.] We've got plenty of food, plenty of towels, plenty of everything! Heh-heh . . ." If you think your mother-in-law is a wreck getting ready to host Thanksgiving dinner, just think how Martha feels entertaining the Son of God. HGTV doesn't have a primer on that.

But in he comes, and they make the best of it: Mary, sitting at his feet as an obedient pupil, drinking in every last word from the Lord's lips, and Martha, scurrying around as a dutiful servant, trying the impossible task of making her home, and herself, a fit habitation for the Messiah. *Get the soup on, set the table, do some quick dusting, make yourself a bit more presentable, light the candles, clean out some cobwebs, how's that soup coming along, fetch the water, and where's Mary?*

The situation is so familiarly human that it's natural to place ourselves in it. For who hasn't been the one who, at suppertime, is left doing all the meal prep or the cleanup—and where in the world are all the supposed helpers? The story of the Little Red Hen is the narrative revenge of Marthas everywhere.

So Martha, taking matters into her own hands, finally goes right to the top, to the Lord himself. She says, "Lord, doesn't it seem unfair to you that my sister just sits here while I do all the work? Tell her to come and *help* me!" (Lk 10:40 NLT, emphasis added). It's an understandable and I'll say reasonable request. But it's also profoundly misguided.

Jesus offers a tender rebuke: "Martha, Martha, you are anxious and troubled about many things, but one thing is necessary. Mary has chosen the good portion, which will not be taken away from her" (Lk 10:41-42).

Now here's where the preacher gets in trouble. It's all too easy to point out Martha's example and say, "See, don't be like Martha, a busybody and worrywart. Instead, be like Mary, and spend time reading your Bible and praying." And the next thing you know, half the Sunday school teachers have put in their two weeks and the men's guild refuses to staff the chili cook-off: if the preacher is telling us that serving is a problem, then there's a simple solution. Not good.

Martha's problem, however, is not merely that she is an overactive helping hand. That can be a wonderful blessing! Her problem is more insidious and altogether more prevalent.

The Martha Complex

The fourth-century church father Hilary of Poitiers diagnosed this problem as *irreligiosa sollicitudo pro Deo*: "the blasphemous anxiety to do God's work for Him."[1] It isn't merely being busy or serving endlessly; those are more symptoms than cause, if anything. Rather, it's trying (fruitlessly) to take over God's business.

You might call it the Martha complex.[2] It's seemingly more benign than a so-called Messiah complex. We're not trying to accomplish eternal salvation for others, after all. Shucks, we'd never do that! No, the Martha complex is less grandiose, and for that reason more sinister. It happens when we try to make God's business our business. And it's by no means restricted to Mary's sister.

In their suggestively titled book *Why It's Okay to Mind Your Own Business*, philosophers Brandon Warmke and Justin Tosi provide a kind of taxonomy of variations to what I'm calling the Martha complex.[3] One is the Moralizer, "the overzealous promoter of his moral beliefs." Moralizers push their piety and pet opinions the way that others do their cell phones, CrossFit gyms, or pyramid schemes. Social media has become a favored arena for the Moralizers. When you moralize you "exceed the proper limits of your role as an enforcer of morality."[4] In other words, you overstep the bounds of your business.

Another perpetrator of the Martha complex is what Warmke and Tosi call the Busybody. Our friendly do-gooder at the cherry shop falls into this category. Scripture critiques this bad habit directly: "For we hear that some among you walk in idleness, not busy at work, but busybodies" (2 Thess 3:11; compare 1 Tim 5:13). And none other than the high-minded philosopher Plato will insist, "To do one's own business and not to be a busybody is justice."[5] While the way we're describing the Martha complex means more than being a busybody, it certainly doesn't mean less.

A third and final brand of the Martha complex, according to Warmke and Tosi, is the Well-meaner. Well-meaners are "those who confidently set out to solve complex problems armed with little more than good intentions." Well-meaners are like Ian Malcolm (played by Jeff Goldblum) in *Jurassic Park*. In one unforgettable scene, the tyrannosaurus is bearing down on young Timmy and Lex, trapped in their Jeep (a decidedly complex problem). Malcolm then apes the clever, informed actions of the paleontologist Dr. Alan Grant, who knew to draw away the T. rex's attention with the use of a flare. Malcolm's well-intentioned but ignorant actions nearly get himself killed. Well-meaners of every sort underrate the nature of the challenge and fail to stay in their proverbial lane.

In many and various ways we thus see the Martha complex playing out in society. But perhaps for Christians it's a special temptation, because it sounds so pious and spiritual. Someone might even object at this point: "Wait a second! Isn't it a *good* thing to make God's business into my business?" You think of young Jesus in the temple. To his bemused parents, he asks, "Did you not know that I must be about my Father's business?" (Lk 2:49 NKJV). Isn't that a question and an attitude that all members of the heavenly family enterprise ought to adopt?

There's an element of truth in this. It is surely the case that we want to follow in the Son's footsteps of joyful submission to the Father. Moreover, the gift of the Spirit, who is the mind of Christ, is melding us to be more like him. So, then, where does this pious obedience turn into blasphemous anxiety? In a world that is off the rails in so many directions, what's really so wrong with the Martha complex?

To answer that question let's consider more closely the cause and the consequences of the complex, which are both much deeper and much darker than the home of a pair of sisters from Bethany.

Diabolical Roots and Shoots

In the middle of the book that bears his name, the prophet Isaiah unleashes a verbal tirade against the King of Tyre that historically the Christian tradition has recognized as having additional *cosmic* significance. Whether he realized it or not, Isaiah may have been telling us something about the devil's origin story:

> How you are fallen from heaven,
>   O Day Star, son of Dawn!
> How you are cut down to the ground,
>   you who laid the nations low!
> You said in your heart,
>   "I will ascend to heaven;
> above the stars of God
>   I will set my throne on high;
> I will sit on the mount of assembly
>   in the far reaches of the north;
> I will ascend above the heights of the clouds;
>   I will make myself like the Most High."
> But you are brought down to Sheol,
>   to the far reaches of the pit. (Is 14:12-15)

The picture that Isaiah gives is of the game we played as kids (and mine still play), King of the Hill. One kid is king atop of the mound or snow berm, and the others are trying to knock him off. Satan was playing cosmic king of the hill. He sought to dethrone the Lord of heaven and earth and lay claim to the universe for himself. He wanted to make God's business his own.

John Milton paints an unforgettable picture of Satan's Martha complex in one of the most well-known passages of *Paradise Lost*:

The mind is its own place, and in itself
Can make a Heaven of Hell, a Hell of Heaven.
What matter where, if I be still the same,
And what I should be, all but less then he
Whom thunder hath made greater? Here at least
We shall be free; the Almighty hath not built
Here for his envy, will not drive us hence:
here we may reign secure, and in my choice
To reign is worth ambition though in Hell:
Better to reign in Hell, than serve in Heaven.[6]

To reign is worth ambition though in hell. Here is the dark heart of the Martha complex. Inasmuch as it manifests as a do-gooding moralizer or even a nosy patron, it appears relatively benign. We could use a few more well-meaning people in a culture that is often, well, *mean*. Given its diabolical roots, however, the Martha complex can clearly have poisonous shoots. We see this play out in the lives of one of Martha's even more famous contemporaries.

Saint Peter is a great hero of the church. He is a martyr who led the incipient body of Christ in its new reality of the Spirit. He was the Rock before Dwayne Johnson came along, and his good confession of Christ resounds through history as a bold and fearless testimony. He was also—and we say it with all affection and admiration—a bit of a doofus. And several moments from his life reveal some of the grievous ramifications of the Martha complex, such that we may need to revise this label.

Preoccupation with purity. Even after Jesus' death, resurrection, and ascension, Peter (and not Peter alone) struggled to shake off a law-oriented preoccupation with purity. He had been there for Jesus' famous "it's not what goes in but what comes out" speech in which, as his buddy Mark observes, "Thus he declared all foods clean" (Mk 7:19). And so God has to give to him a special, dramatic vision of the animals and the sheet—three times! (Acts 10:16). The Lord tells him, "Do not declare unclean what I have called clean." In other words, quit trying to tell me how to do my job, Peter. But it's hard not to sympathize with Peter; so profound was this transformation of worldview, most everyone failed to grasp it at first—both then and thereafter.

The church has struggled with this through the ages. One of the most dramatic instances was in the fourth-century schism known as Donatism, named for the bishop Donatus who insisted that the effectiveness of the sacraments depended on the worthiness of the minister. The schism arose out of a time of persecution, when many Christians (including Christian leaders) compromised their confession to save their skin. Donatists asserted that the church must be pure of such fickle faithful; only true believers need apply.

The Donatists possessed an admirable rigor, and their concerns about compromised Christians were not totally unfounded. Even so, as Saint Augustine powerfully countered, their preoccupation with purity in itself compromised the gospel of grace. Theologian Ben Quash writes, "It is God's job to make the Church pure, not ours, and he will do it when he is ready. However morally zealous we are, we will never by our own effort carve out a pure space which we can call the true Church by pointing to the unimpeachable lives of its members."[7] Like Peter, they needed to learn again, as his interlocutor Paul insisted, "nothing is unclean in itself" (Rom 14:14).

Righteous rage. Peter was PO'd. And understandably so. He had just witnessed one of his own fellow apostles, one of his brothers-in-arms, hand over their rabbi to the religious authorities. Consequently, Peter decided to take matters into his own hands. Contrary to his Lord's instructions, Peter unsheathed his sword and swung at one of the high priest's henchmen—a poor sap called Malchus (Jn 18:10). Whether due to exquisite aim or laughable error, Peter managed to slice off Malchus's ear. Jesus promptly repaired the ear and swiveled to Peter: "Put your sword into its sheath; shall I not drink the cup that the Father has given me?" (Jn 18:11). Another of the common consequences of the Martha complex is righteous rage that seeks to take matters into your own hands. In that moment, Peter—moved with anger—tried to do God's work for him. It could only end badly.

But let's give an example of this that's closer to where many of us live or have lived: parenting. In his book *Scream-Free Parenting*, family therapist Hal Runkel recounts a visit to the Waffle House with his family that went horribly awry. It was a Saturday morning and the place was busy beyond belief. The Runkel family's server, bless her heart, gave some crayons and paper hats to try and mollify the increasingly hangry kids. Once the food finally came to the table, though, Runkel's two-year-old son, Brandon, simply wouldn't be satisfied. What's more, in his devilish toddler mind, he seemed to notice that his tantrum was gaining the attention of the fellow patrons. So he had the ingenious idea to throw the whole waffle, plate and all, on to the floor. The plate broke, syrup splattered, people gasped, Brandon screamed . . . and dad lost his cool. Runkel narrates the scene:

> All eyes were fixed on us as my son kept screaming. And kicking. And hitting. I was seething as I pushed the door open with such force that it rattled glass walls. The reverberating structure got everyone's attention. So now, whoever wasn't watching this scene unfold inside the restaurant was now watching from the inside as I stood there on the sidewalk, yelling at my son. I was using big words, asking rhetorical questions, puffing out my chest, pointing my finger, and intimidating a boy who couldn't have stood more than thirty-six inches tall.

It was in that moment that Runkel also realized that he was still wearing one of the paper Waffle House hats.

Reflecting on his anxious attempt to control his son, Runkel writes, "The reason we feel so overwhelmed now, is because most of us are attempting to follow an impossible mindset. And this mindset is fueled by a dangerous lie, a lie so embedded in our social consciousness that it sounds crazy to question it."[8] That lie, as Runkel goes on to tell it, is that we assume personal responsibility for every action of our kids. This can only lead to frustration, anger, screaming. "Something happens and you take it personally, you get upset," says psychologist David Lieberman, author of *Never Get Angry Again*. "Something happens and you *don't* take it personally, you don't get upset. That's twenty-five years of therapy in a sentence."[9] The blasphemous anxiety often manifests itself as biting anger.

Prideful comparing. A further consequence of the Martha complex is that you are prone to prideful comparing. Here, consider a moment at the end of John's Gospel. It's a tender moment of reconciliation . . . in which Peter can't help once again to put his foot in his mouth. Jesus has just offered him absolution for his triple denial by way of a renewed summons to follow him. But no sooner does Jesus say that to him then Peter turns around to look at John, "the disciple whom Jesus loved." And he can't help himself. "Lord," he asks, "what about this man?" *Hey, this forgiveness and promise to lead your church is great and all, but what's up with this other guy?* Jesus won't abide it, however. "If it is my will that he remain until I come, what is that to you?" he says, perhaps an edge detected in his voice. "You follow me!" (Jn 21:22).

This scene is dramatically adapted at the end of *The Voyage of the Dawn Treader* from the Narnia series. The Pevensey children have just learned from Aslan the lion, king of Narnia, that they won't be returning to that blessed country. Their first reaction is distress at the thought that they will not see Aslan again, a concern he assuages at once. As humans are so wont to do, however, they promptly pivot to comparison: "And is Eustace never to come back here either?" said Lucy. (Echoes of Peter are unmistakable.) But Aslan, as the figure of Jesus, tenderly responds: "'Child,' said Aslan, 'do you really need to know that? Come, I am opening the door in the sky.'"[10]

The Martha complex can't help comparing. It always wants to stick its nose into other people's business. That old blasphemous anxiety at work once more.

Theodicy: Protecting God from God. One last consequence of the Martha complex that bears mentioning is particularly prevalent amongst preachers and theologians. It's the knee-jerk attempt to defend God, commonly known as "theodicy," which is a fancy term that in practice can seem to mean something like "sophisticated strategies for getting God off the hook."

This is evident in what is arguably Peter's lowest moment (his denials notwithstanding); it occurs fast on the heels of his highest. To Jesus' pointed question, "Who do you say I am?" Peter responds with bold and unflinching faith: "You are the Christ, the Son of the living God!" (Mt 16:16). Bravo, Pete! You nailed it![11] But in the next breath, Jesus begins telling the disciples of his impending suffering, death, and—note well—resurrection (evidently no one was able to hear this latter part). And straight away, like a dashing white knight, Peter rushes to Jesus' aid, going so far as to rebuke Jesus for his poor theology. "Far be it from you, Lord! This shall never happen to you!" (Mt 16:22). It's a precious bit of disciple-splaining. *You know, Lord, this is just not the way that these things work. Get with the program.*

Jesus has his own, cruciform program, and therefore promptly puts Peter back in his place. "Get behind me, Satan! You are a hindrance to me. For you are not setting your mind on the things of God, but on the things of man!" (Mt 16:23). In his anxious attempts to co-opt God's business, Peter is not only blasphemous; he's downright diabolical.

Truly, the Martha complex needs to add to its namesake the preeminent apostle.

The Perils of Visionary Dreaming

Underlying the blasphemous anxiety of the Martha-Peter complex is the quest for control. That's why people will so often turn to anger, comparisons, even vengeance. Our most natural prayer is, "Lord, let *my* will be done." We offer it up implicitly whenever we fight and scrape to have our way. Though as adults we might not throw temper tantrums like a toddler, it's not because the impulse is overcome, just under wraps. Our nastiness is more nuanced. And it's when life feels most uncontrollable that we tend to double down on the quest for control and the worst tendencies of the Martha-Peter complex.

What, then, is the prognosis? As you would expect for a syndrome with such unholy ties, it's bleak. Dietrich Bonhoeffer hits on this in his classic book of Christian community, *Life Together*. It might not be surprising that a book about community would commend the virtues of minding your own business. But Bonhoeffer doesn't just bemoan busybodies. He saw clearly the deeper, more dastardly side of the blasphemous anxiety—and its profound consequences.

Bonhoeffer punches right between the eyes what is regarded as one of the unarguable necessities of the Christian life, certainly the life of the Christian community: *vision*. He writes, "God hates visionary dreaming; it makes the dreamer proud and pretentious. The man who fashions a visionary ideal of community demands that it be realized by God, by others, and by himself."[12] This is not to say that there isn't a place for prayerfully developing a picture of "God's better future" for us or our church, as one author defines vision.[13] Bonhoeffer's point is rather that such visions need to be held lightly, susceptible as they are to the limitations of the blasphemous anxiety. We butt into God's business and demand our dream be realized by him. My will be done once again.

Bonhoeffer sees clearly where such ambitions lead, however, for the one who is in the throes of the blasphemous anxiety. "When things do not go his way," he writes, "he calls the effort a failure." He continues: "When his ideal picture is destroyed, he sees the community going to smash. So he becomes, first an accuser of his brethren, then an accuser of God, and finally the despairing accuser of himself."[14]

In this chapter we've examined a pair of biblical characters in Martha and Peter and seen how both of them succumbed to varying degrees to the temptation to try and do God's work for him. Bonhoeffer's comments point toward one final example, the most grievous one of all: Judas.

The question of why Judas, one of Jesus' handpicked apostles, would betray his Lord has addled Christians across the centuries.

The biblical testimony is notably quiet on this score. Some have suggested that simple greed drove him; after all, John notes that Judas was reputed to be a thief. Others propose that he was motivated by jealousy, having been left out of the inner ring of the apostles. And still others that he was merely an unwitting prop of fate and possessed by Satan to do the evil one's bidding. There are merits in each of these explanations, and I don't rule out any of them entirely.

More compelling to me, however, and I believe more consonant with the biblical evidence, is that Judas was trying to force Jesus' hand. Like so many expectant sons of Israel in his day (including other apostles), he had a vision of who the Messiah would be and the kind of kingdom he would bring about. At every turn, Jesus frustrated those expectations. He came not in power but in weakness, not in vengeance but in mercy. He did not summarily depose Caesar and, as the slow-learning disciples solicited on the day of his ascension, "restore the kingdom to Israel" (Acts 1:6). He didn't just get down to business.

Perhaps, then, it has been suggested, Judas resolved to take matters into his own hands. If his rabbi will not carry out God's business, then—like a stubborn toddler refusing his parents help—*I'll do it myself!* Hand over Jesus, precipitate the final showdown, summon legions of angel armies, and bring this kingdom once and for all. Or so he may have imagined.[15]

In short, maybe we should have called this the Judas complex. Because herein is the most egregious outcome of that blasphemous anxiety. To be sure, God works all things according to his will, and what was intended for evil he used for good. And yet, for Judas, there was no path back from that pit of despair. In thrall to Satan, that ancient accuser, Judas became (as Bonhoeffer wrote), the accuser of his brethren, the accuser of God, and finally the despairing accuser of himself.

The issue with the blasphemous anxiety is not that it makes you a Karen, but that it leads back into the slough of despond that we have dubbed quiet desperation. If it is up to you and me to see to it that God's business is done, we are lost. But as it is, we have a more hopeful, life-giving ambition: to tend our own business—and let God tend his. To that we now turn.

6

GOD'S BUSINESS AND OURS

THERE'S AN OLD JOKE that theologians like to tell. That probably tells you all you need to know about its comedic value, but here goes.

Saint Peter is manning the pearly gates when three men approach his booth in the midst of a heated debate. "Gentlemen," Peter says, "why should you be received into your heavenly home?" (This being a theologians' joke, there are usually some caveats here about how this is not at all how it goes when one enters into eternal life, but I'll spare you any more pedantry.)

"Well," says the first, stepping up with a great big sack over his shoulder, "this is just what we were discussing."

"And for the record, you are, sir?"

"I am Thomas of Aquinas. And I have with me here my massive sack of good works. For I know that unless a life is marked by virtuous deeds, it will by no means be pleasing to God."

At this point a second fellow steps forth with a pointy beard, a floppy hat, and a still larger sack. "And I, dear Peter, am Ulrich Zwingli. And my esteemed colleague here is much too in the thrall of Aristotle. My sack is not filled with virtuous deeds but with radical acts of obedience to Christ. That's what truly makes me acceptable to God and worthy of heaven."

The third, rather portly, participant of this curious triad hung in the back with a look of consternation on his face. His sack sat lifelessly at his side, evidently empty.

"And you there," summoned Saint Peter. "Who are you? And what have you in your sack?"

"Dear Peter, I am Martin Luther, and I've come with an empty sack."

A wry smile creeps across the apostle's face. "You mean to tell me you haven't brought all your good works for admission to heaven? No virtuous deeds, no radical acts?"

"No, sir," Luther says, just standing there. "I come as a beggar, trusting only in the mercy of the Savior. And my sack is empty because I left all my good works with my neighbors on earth."[1]

I told you Dave Chapelle isn't going to add it to his set any time soon. But what this little story lacks in comedy it makes up for in substance, because it points to the heart of the next part of the quiet ambition: "tend your own business." As we'll see in this chapter, this speaks to what is our proper business, what is God's, and how these two hold together.

Knowing Your Proper Place

But just what does Saint Paul mean by "tend your own business"? The phrase itself can be misleading, and it's important both to situate it in our broader context as well as to look more closely at the words themselves. That sounds a little dry, but bear with me, there's some gold in them thar hills.

First, recall that the quiet ambition is a way that hope takes shape each day, finding the largeness in littleness. We saw in chapter five with the Martha complex that the "blasphemous anxiety" to nose ourselves into God's business leads only to frustration, anger, and finally despair—the no-hope state of mind. That attitude needs to be flipped on its head. We need to recover a sense of what's God's business, and what's ours as his human creatures. By keeping that proper distinction, we'll pave the pathway for hope.

But second, we need to talk about this phrase "tend your own business"—or, as it's commonly translated, *mind* your own business—because it can carry with it some connotations that are neither biblical nor altogether helpful. When I hear it, I can't help thinking of the turf wars that daily ensue in my house among my kids. One of them might be reading a book on the couch when her sister leans over to see what she's looking at, only to elicit the protest, "Hey, mind your own business!" Or one of the boys might have some project he's toiling away at in the basement when his younger sister starts poking around, asking questions, offering unsolicited advice, until finally he gives an impatient eye roll with, "Mind your own business, okay?" Is *this* the attitude that the Scriptures are talking about?

A friend of mine who's a retired teacher has a motto he likes to trot out when we start talking about matters of his old school: "Not my circus, not my monkeys." (He's got it on a bumper sticker, in fact; I'm not sure which came first, the sticker or his motto—or indeed the circus or the monkeys. But I digress.) It's a funny and occasionally useful quip—but is *this* what Paul means by "tend your own business"?

My kids and my retired friend are touching on something significant. There's plenty to be said for simply knowing your place and, in the variant translation of my youth, "minding your own beeswax." Speaking of alternate translations, though, it's worth revisiting the phrase in its original language, because this will open the door to seeing a deeper and richer understanding to this element of the unambitious ambition.

In the Greek of the New Testament, Paul's admonition is startlingly terse and to the point. What's fascinating is that there is not an inkling of "minding." Paul has vocabulary to say such a thing and uses it regularly (e.g., Phil 2:5; Rom 12:2). But what comes to mind with "minding" is brain matters: thinking and reflecting and cogitating. The verb that is used in 1 Thessalonians 4:11, though, is not about *cognition* but *action*: *prassein* is the root for our English word "practice" and is typically translated as "do" or "act." The NASB translation gets closer when it says, "Attend to your own business." More straightforward still is the old KJV: "Do your own business."

What difference does this make? I think it can reframe our understanding of what the apostle is summoning us to. It's not merely about minding your own beeswax and keeping your nose out of others' business—necessary as that advice can sometimes be (for parents and otherwise). It's more about knowing your proper place and answering what's asked of you. (In other words, this is a matter of vocation, a topic that we will look at more closely later in the book.)

Furthermore, there is both a passive and an active side to tending your own business: receiving God's labor on your behalf, on the one hand, and on the other responding with your own labor on behalf of your neighbors. This distinction makes all the difference.

God's Business on Our Behalf

God is in the business of redeeming, renewing, and restoring his creation. For us to tend our own business, then, means first and foremost to step back and allow him to carry out his. *Let God cook.*

Think of the story of the exodus and in particular the crossing of the Red Sea. To this point the Lord has been single-handedly bringing the Israelites out of Egypt; their only contribution is their stubbornness. They have dragged their feet and stiffened their neck. Even so, true to his promise, God has laid low Pharaoh and blazed a trail to freedom for his "firstborn son" (Ex 4:22), the children of Israel.

But for all this—the plagues, the Passover, the escape from Egypt—Israel is not convinced and Pharaoh is not dissuaded. It all comes to a head on the banks of the Red Sea. With the jilted king of Egypt and his army breathing with hot breath down their necks, the people start crying out and turning downright nasty. "Is it because there are no graves in Egypt that you have taken us away to die in the wilderness? What have you done to us in bringing us out of Egypt? . . . It would have been better for us to serve the Egyptians than to die in the wilderness" (Ex 14:11-12). It's a remarkable bit of hubris, not to mention amnesia.

Be that as it may, Moses' response tells us everything about God's business:

> Fear not, stand firm, and see the salvation of the Lord, which he will work for you today. For the Egyptians whom you see today, you shall never see again. The Lord will fight for you, and you have only to be silent. (Ex 14:13-14)

I appreciate the subtle dig at the end there: Can you please just shut your traps? But it carries a profound point: God doesn't need help delivering you. He's fighting on your behalf. He's responsible for your rescue. And what do you have to do? "Be silent." Behold his salvation. Receive from him.

God's business is deliverance, mercy, and rescue. This is his proper work; it is right there at the top of his job description. Divine monergism is the fancy theological term: "one-work-ism." Theologian Paul Zahl calls it God's "one-way love."[2] The apostle Paul proclaims it again and again in his New Testament Epistles, in particular Romans and Galatians. For instance, Romans: "But God shows his love for us in that while we were still sinners, Christ died for us" (Rom 5:8). I never tire of preaching that Jesus' dying words from the cross were not, "It's mostly done—can you take it from here?" but "It is *finished*." Complete. Done. For you.

So where things get muddled is when we humans fail to stay in our spiritual lane, so to speak. Earlier generations of the church repudiated heresies such as Pelagianism, which touted a bald-faced synergism ("work-together-ism") that mingled God's business and ours. "Well, yes, God does a lot to save us," Pelagians said, "but we've got the power to save ourselves too!" To the contrary, responded great theologians like Augustine, there are no arms on earth strong enough to lift ourselves up by these sin-riddled bootstraps. Mercifully, the most flagrant forms of this heresy were formally denounced by orthodox Christians. Variations nevertheless spring up from age to age like stubborn weeds.

This was what got Martin Luther and the other reformers all riled up in the late Middle Ages. They saw in the increasingly complicated machinations of the Roman church a kind of "semi-Pelagianism" that had human merit laying claim to the gift of salvation. It was "half-way love." To the contrary, Luther insisted, salvation comes ever and always *sola gratia*, by grace alone. Hence, in the story that opened this chapter, he's just a beggar with an empty sack. In the immortal words of the hymn "Rock of Ages": "Nothing in my hands I bring, / simply to Thy cross I cling."[3]

God's business is unilateral rescue and salvation. He is "the Father of lights," from whom comes "every good gift and every perfect gift" (Jas 1:17). Every last one. And Jesus has followed in the family train. As he posed the question to his surprised parents: "Did you not know that I must be about my Father's business?" (Lk 2:49 NKJV). Yahweh and Son is up and running, and business is good. "My Father has been working until now, and I have been working" (Jn 5:17).

Recognizing God's proper business therefore enables us to tend to our own business: receiving and responding.

Receiving from the Lord

In the story of the two sisters that we looked at in chapter five, Martha stands out. It's easy for the anecdote merely to become a cautionary tale about the perils of unbounded busyness. But if we don't pay heed to her sister, we miss Jesus' primary point. The Martha complex is hazardous, but the way of Mary is salutary.

Mary is a paragon of living quietly. In the history of the church she has often been portrayed as the icon of the *vita contemplativa*, the contemplative life. This is all well and good. But we don't need to overstate her virtue or lionize her legacy, because that undermines what's significant about what Mary does here. Which is to say: not much.

As Martha flits to and fro, all we are told is that Mary "sat at the Lord's feet and listened to his teaching" (Lk 10:39; the Greek for "listen intently" is *ekouen*, an intensive imperfect). Her posture is pure receptivity. Like Luther, you might say that she is a beggar. But in the economy of God's kingdom, a beggar is a blessed person. What stands out about Mary, then, is not so much what she's doing as what she's *not* doing: usurping the Lord's work. Instead, she attends to her business, which is first and foremost to receive the good gifts that he wishes to give. As Jesus says, this is the "one thing [that] is necessary." Receiving from the Lord is our day job, if you like, as his beloved creatures.

Jesus is persistent on this point. Take one of the most outrageous and illuminating exchanges that he has with the disciples. A pair of them, James and John, enlist the help of their mom (!) in order to jockey for pole position in the kingdom of God. "Grant us to sit at your right hand and at your left" is how they piously put it to Jesus. But the Lord can see it for the naked ambition that it is and says—if

I can paraphrase—*Listen, guys, the Gentiles are always scrapping and clawing to get ahead, to get a leg up, but that's not how we work. Instead, our mobility will be downward. Our ambition will be unambitious.* And then this profound point, which drives home the passive posture of his followers: "The Son of Man came not to be served but to serve, and to give his life as a ransom for many" (Mt 20:28). Jesus' job, which he came for and delights in, is to *serve.* Uncomfortable as it can sometimes feel for us inveterate Marthas (and Peters), our business before anything else is simply to be served by Christ.

Nor should we disregard the receptivity of faith itself. Sometimes faith can be positioned as the preeminent work: the one accomplishment that we get to claim. Yet even the fact that we believe it is a gift. In his novel *The Hammer of God*, author Bo Giertz provides an unforgettable image for this passivity of faith. The novel tells the story of Fridfeldt—a brash, young pastor who is impressed with his own devotion—and his sage aged mentor (simply called "the rector"), whom the younger man regards as being a little too lax and reliant on grace for his own good.

Early in their relationship, Fridfeldt puts his cards on the table. "I just want you to know from the beginning, sir, that I am a believer." The rector takes up the gauntlet in stride. "So you're a believer," he says, "I'm glad to hear that. What do you believe in?"

This puts Fridfeldt back on his heels. Doesn't it go without saying? "In Jesus, of course," he insists. "I mean—I mean I have given him my heart." At this, the old rector turns solemn. You get the sense from his reaction that he is concerned that this young buck is migrating from zeal to presumption. "Do you consider that something to give him?" the rector asks.

By now, Fridfeldt is beside himself. "But sir, if you do not give your heart to Jesus you cannot be saved!" And here the rector comes in with the *coup de grace*:

> You are right, my boy. And it is just as true that, if you think you are saved *because* you give Jesus your heart, you will not be saved. You see, my boy, it is one thing to choose Jesus as one's Lord and Savior, to give him one's heart and commit oneself to him, and that he now accepts one into his little flock; it is a very different thing to believe on him as a Redeemer of sinners, of whom one is chief. One does not choose a Redeemer for oneself, you understand, nor give one's heart to him. The heart is a rusty old can on a junk heap. A fine birthday gift, indeed! But a wonderful Lord passes by, and has mercy on the wretched tin can, sticks his walking cane through it, and rescues it from the junk pile and takes it home with him. That is how it is.[4]

That is indeed how it is. There are good works for us to do; the life of faith is ever busy and active. But we must recognize that our principal posture, our basic business, is receptivity. The Lord would have us tend to this business by, like Mary, attending to his words, accepting his gifts, acquiescing to his good and gracious will. That's ever and always where it starts: in the span of a life, when he first takes hold of us through the gospel; in the span of a week, when we gather together on the Lord's Day with our fellow beggars to receive his blessed bread; in the span of a day, when we awaken with crusties in our eyes and a frog in our throat and remember, once again, that the Savior who came to serve and not to be served loves me in this, my unpolished self, apart from any merit or worthiness in me.

That's ever and always where it starts, I say: with receptivity. But that's not where it stops. Therefore, we also get down to business by responding to what we have received with "faith working through love" (Gal 5:6).

Loving Labor for the Neighbor

On the one hand, tending means *surrendering*: letting God be God for us. But on the other hand, tending means *contending*: fighting for the people, projects, and places the Lord has put into your path. This is the significance in the joke of Martin Luther saying that he left his good works on earth with others, because God doesn't need them, but your neighbor does. So Chad Bird writes poetically, "The opposite of ambition is not laziness or apathy. The opposite of ambition is loving labor on behalf of the neighbor."[5]

This is important to recognize, because as I have suggested there's a way of understanding "mind your own business" that further isolates us and exacerbates our already hyperindividualistic tendencies. *I'm just going to get mine, mind my own, put my head down, let others worry about themselves.* This is emphatically *not* the message of the unambitious ambition. Tending your own business entails "loving labor on behalf of the neighbor." In English and in Greek, "neighbor" literally means *near-person*. Or you might say, "the nearby-guy": the one whom the Lord has set before you.

The famous story of the good Samaritan is instructive here (Lk 10:25-37). You've got the man who gets sideswiped by some hoodlums on his way home. He's face-down in a ditch, left for dead. It's a grave situation. But, as Jesus tells us, a priest soon comes along. He sees the half-dead man and thinks, *Not my circus, not my monkeys.* And then a pious lay leader from church saddles up; he leans in to have a look, but thinks, *I just need to mind my own beeswax.* Meanwhile, the last trace of hope is seeping out of our friend in the ditch.

But then a Samaritan passes by, and this fellow, Jesus says, "came to where he was, and when he saw him, he had compassion." He tended to the business placed right in front of him. He did what he could to get the man into more promising straits, patching him up, taking him to a safe haven, even covering a night's stay and some square meals. The Samaritan didn't hover over him like a mother bird or anxiously assume responsibility for the man's future; that wasn't his job. But he did show care.

And Jesus asks, the cat fully out of the bag, "Which of these three seemed to be a neighbor to the man waylaid by the bandits?" It's the one who showed loving labor on behalf of his neighbor. The Samaritan, who tended to the business God set before him.

I marvel at the everyday saints whom God has given me the opportunity to minister to. Folks who have imbibed what it means to go about the business that God has given them, who practice the unambitious ambition as second nature. For instance, I think of Cal. Cal was on the margins of our parish. He never darkened the door of the church on Sunday morning to my knowledge, but in a small town like where I was serving at the time—where there's only one church for the community—you're effectively part of the parish even when you don't belong to the worshiping community.

Cal operates a tow-truck service—the kind of unglamorous yet absolutely essential work in which you'll often find practitioners of quiet ambition. In my first couple of years in the parish I got to know Cal in this capacity well, because I'd thought it would be a good idea to get a truck befitting the rugged rural area. (I don't want to cast aspersions on any particular brand, but I'll just say it rhymed with *sheep*.) The first time I met Cal, I had been cruising down the highway, a scenic two-lane road that hugs Lake Michigan, when suddenly the transfer case on my four-wheel-drive grenaded out from under me and I puttered helplessly to the side of the road. Cal came with a tow in short order. He didn't give me the hard time I expected, but just tied up my rig and invited me to grab shotgun for the ride home.

I'm ashamed to admit it, but when I first saw Cal my prejudice prevailed on me. Here's a thirty-something fellow decked out in his Carhartts and fishnet ballcap, with a beard that would make Grizzly Adams envious, and I thought, *Great, I've got to get back home, and now I'm counting on this bumpkin to help me out.* I tried to make small talk as we drove; he was a man of few words. At one point, we narrowly missed a whole herd of deer as Cal was checking his phone for his next job. When I asked if he ever hit any, he just winked and assured me that his industrial strength bumper could plow through a dozen of them without us even noticing.

That got us on the topic of his truck. He mentioned that he'd only had it a year, that he had to replace his last one, "a real beaut." "So why'd you replace it?" I asked. He told me that he got into a *pret-ty* bad accident—which, as it turns out, was like saying that the Hindenburg had a minor explosion.

My curiosity got the better of me and I asked him the story. Cal smacked his lips and began to tell it as dispassionately as if he were recounting his morning's breakfast. He says that he was driving down county line road in the middle of the night when this little four-door started swerving around and coming at him. There was no shoulder on the road so he just held his line; he knew his truck would win any chicken fights.

The car gets real close, Cal says, and he can see that the gal behind the wheel is passed out. He would come to find out she had OD'd, probably on opioids. Well, he says, he braced himself for impact and the car hit him head-on. (I'm thinking to myself, in the immortal words of Ron Burgundy in *Anchorman*: *This escalated quickly*.) I assume it's the end of the story, so I try to fill in the rest: "So the crash totaled your truck," I offer. Not quite, Cal says.

The impact knocks Cal out for a second, and when he comes to he finds that his door is jammed shut. He looks out his windshield and sees that the car is on fire and the other driver is face-down on the steering wheel in a bad way. By this time I'm on the edge of my seat: turns out the bumpkin's got a story to tell, I think to myself. Despite my efforts to try and play it cool, my reaction betrayed my amazement.

"Yep, it was bad, real bad," Cal says. He seemed content to stop the story there, but I could tell there was still more to it. I asked what he did next.

Cal took a big breath and rubbed the back of his neck. Then he related how he climbed out the broken window—and that's when he heard the crying. I interrupt: "I thought you said the lady was dead." Cal says, "Yep, she was: dead as a doornail. But the crying was coming from the back seat." An eight-month-old little baby was stuck in its car seat, unharmed by the collision but imperiled by the fire. And that's when Cal hopped to it. With a rush of adrenaline, he breaks the sedan's back window, climbs in, and pulls the baby out safe and sound. (She now lives with her father and all is apparently well.)

Within moments, both the car and Cal's tow truck were immolated.

"Anyhow, that's why I had to get a new truck," he concluded matter-of-factly.

By now my jaw is on the floor. One minute I was judging this guy for being a yokel, the next minute I'm in awe of him. It was clear that Cal had no mind for boasting, but that didn't mean I couldn't prod him. "Dude! You're a hero!" I said.

"Nah," he says, eyes forward down the road. "Just handlin' my business. Wasn't nothing that nobody else wouldn't do."

Cal's heroic actions were extraordinary, and Lord willing none of us will find ourselves in such an extreme, life-and-death situation. But it's his humble attitude and modest appraisal of his good deed—not to mention how gracefully and capably he did his job—that, to me, makes for such a powerful picture of what it looks like to tend your own business.

Had he been out patrolling the roads, like Batman looking for trouble that he had to fix—more horrific accidents where he needed to save a damsel in distress—it would be a severe case of the Martha complex. As it is, he simply sought to ply his trade and be of use to people in need. He possessed the peaceful posture, the easygoing spirit, of someone who understands God's work and his own. *Just handlin' my business.*

The Anti-Creed

This peaceful spirit is ours as baptized and beloved children of God who live in the rhythm of receiving from him and responding with care for others. One thing I've found that can help keep this rhythm is to profess the "Anti-Creed."

A friend of mine named Greg Finke gave me this phrase.[6] We were talking about John the Baptist. You recall how, at one time, the religious leaders caught wind that John was out baptizing people and heralding God's coming kingdom. They pester him: "Who are you, anyway?" And John responds unequivocally: "He confessed, and did not deny, but confessed, 'I am not the Christ'" (Jn 1:20). And Greg says, "It's the Anti-Creed!"

In the traditional creeds of the church we confess (and do not deny) who we believe God to be. The Anti-Creed turns this on its head, confessing who and what we *don't* believe about *ourselves*. So, hand over your heart, scout's honor, join me in confessing.

I do *not* believe . . .

. . . that I am the Christ.

. . . that I can solve the world's problems.

. . . that I must justify God to the world.

. . . that I have to sift the sinners from the saints.

. . . that I need to correct every incorrect opinion.

. . . that I must determine heaven's guest list.

And so on. You can insert your own articles of belief—or unbelief, as it were. The bottom line is that, with John the Baptist, we embrace our creaturely limitations and let God be God for us. As John also said: Jesus must increase, we must decrease (Jn 3:30). That's truly good news.

Pastor and author Jon Tyson, writing about the blessings and challenges of aging, gets at the gifts of letting God be God. He writes,

> There is a kind of glorious freedom in acknowledging our weaknesses and limitations as we age. A joy in not having to be everywhere, do everything, fix everyone, show up as the expert, solve all the problems. There is a new confidence and humility that emerges through a sober assessment about what we are good at, what we are called to, and what actually fills the heart.[7]

Glorious freedom. That's what we have been given in the finished work of Jesus on our behalf. You and I don't have to be the Savior; that job has been filled to perfection. Instead, we can find the largeness in the little things put in our path (which are often not so little after all) and leave the rest to the Lord. As Luther simply put it, "Pray, and let God worry."[8] That's his business, and business is good.

The Practice of Tending Your Own Business

We are all susceptible to the blasphemous anxiety to attempt to do God's work for him. Like Martha and Peter, we can confuse the Lord's business for our own. The invitation of the quiet ambition is instead to "tend your own business," living in the rhythm of receiving and responding. God is God and you are not; that's a good thing.

Suggestions for practicing the quiet ambition

1. **Make sabbath essential.** Sabbath literally means stop, and fittingly it comes at the *start* of our weeks. We imitate Mary by first attending to the Lord's word and receiving his gifts; our work then flows from God's work.
   - Weekly worship attendance is the "keystone habit" to a restful sabbath. And remember: Jesus is there to serve you, not the other way around.
   - Don't let Sunday become a "junk-drawer day" that random tasks and responsibilities get thrown into. That's why God gave you Saturday!
   - Adopt slow-cooker Sunday. Throw a roast in the crock pot before worship so that you can relax in the afternoon before enjoying a delicious meal, preferably with family or friends.
2. **Confess the Anti-Creed.** A missionary friend used to wake up in the morning, get out of bed, look himself in the mirror

and repeat, "I don't have to do anything today." It was his version of the Anti-Creed. We would do well to adopt a similar habit.

- Reflect on John the Baptist's Anti-Creed. In what ways are you tempted to act as though you were the Christ, rescuing the world? What is keeping you worried and anxious, as Martha was? Jot out some thoughts that you can offer up to the Lord.
- Write out the Apostles' Creed, and then add alongside it your own version of the Anti-Creed. Post it beside your bathroom mirror. You might include the glad admission of the Baptizer, "Christ must increase, and I must decrease."

3. **Submit to God's control.** Jesus is Lord. He is in control, I am not. The spiritual discipline of submission is the humble recognition that Christ is the vine, we are the branches, and apart from him we can't do anything (Jn 15). How can you put this into practice?
   - Reflect on Jesus' prayer in the Garden of Gethsemane (Mt 26:36-46). What strikes you about his submission? Meditate on an artistic rendering or icon of this scene.
   - A pious habit of old that is ripe for recovery is the signing of correspondence D.V.—*Deo volente*, "If God wills." Try adding this to your email signature when appropriate.
   - Along similar lines, you might "sign" your petitions to the Lord, "Thy will, not mine, be done." We can't be reminded enough!
4. **Subscribe to "slow media."** Social media, cable news, and the churn of the twenty-four-hour news cycle aggravate the worst tendencies of the Martha complex. "Thou shalt stay

up-to-date and in-the-loop" is an oppressive, unbiblical injunction that I recommend breaking as often and vehemently as possible. Subscribe to the weekly edition of the old-fashioned newspaper instead. You can read it while the slow-cooker makes dinner on Sunday afternoon.

5. **WAIT:** A friend taught me this acronym for teaching: "Why Am I Talking?" You don't always have to add your two cents. Practicing restraint with the tongue is a salutary habit. We could also revise this to be "Why Am I Tending?" It is a helpful diagnostic question to ask when you find yourself getting tied up in others' business.

Part 4

WORK WITH YOUR HANDS

7

POLISHING FORKS FOR THE KINGDOM

"We work with our heads," remarked the estimable British wit Samuel Johnson in the 1700s, "and make the boobies of Birmingham work for us with their hands."[1] Everyone who's anyone, he's saying, keeps their hands clean of work that would make their hands dirty. His attitude toward manual labor was hardly novel and it continues largely unabated to this day.

From age to age, those who work with their hands have been regarded as inferior to those who, as Dr. Johnson put it, "work with [their] heads." The assumption of first-century Greco-Roman culture was that the life well lived was the life of the mind. Manual labor was menial labor, reserved for slaves and children. Inasmuch as Christianity was thought to be a philosophy, a life-orienting system of beliefs and practices, it would have been expected that its adherents devote their days to contemplation. The Roman satirist Lucian, for example, commented on (and critiqued) the commonplace habit of craftsmen abandoning their trade after converting to philosophy. Serious philosophers insisted that they were following a "higher calling" than mere tradesmen.[2] Aristotle states it bluntly: "We think that the masterworkers in each craft are more honorable and know in a truer sense and are wiser than the manual workers."[3]

Many of today's cultural conditions have changed from the time of the New Testament, but the biased attitude toward working with your hands largely has not. For example, a yawning skilled labor gap has opened in our society due to the many retiring baby boomers, making jobs in the trades more lucrative than ever. Even so, far too few young people are going that route.[4] In a report on blue-collar careers issued in 2023 by the website Jobber, 74 percent of respondents said that they think there is a stigma associated with going to a trade school over a traditional four-year university, and 79 percent of respondents said their parents want them to pursue a college education after high school; only 5 percent said the same about vocational school.[5]

This denigration of manual labor has real ramifications for countless people, Christians included. As Brian Dijkema writes,

> It's nice to say "it's so good that you care for our elderly," but it's much harder to talk about having to change colostomy bags, or how you smell when you're done cleaning out a chicken barn. Yet this work takes the waking hours of many people—perhaps even the majority—in North America and certainly the world. Leaving this work out of the conversation not only leaves too many on the outside, but unwittingly communicates a certain hopelessness, as if joy and satisfaction—indeed the Lord's satisfaction—cannot be found in this type of work.[6]

For such workers devoid of affirmation, quiet desperation abounds.

We're exploring the quiet ambition and how hope takes shape in everyday life. In this chapter we begin our look at the next part of Paul's paradoxical program, considering how it is that the apostle can encourage his readers—with the force of Holy Writ and divine inspiration behind him—to "work with your hands." Implicit in the proposition is that manual labor, whether it's the work of farmers or nursing home attendants, diesel mechanics or septic operators, can in fact bring joy and satisfaction to the Lord and his people alike; that it has not only cultural or economic worth but in fact possesses *spiritual* value.

But of course many of us, perhaps most, don't receive our daily bread from the toil and moil of our mitts—unless those mitts are grading papers, tapping on a keyboard, or packing a kid's lunch. Does Scripture's summons to work with our hands speak to us too?

I believe that it does. Inquiring into the spiritual value of manual labor, it turns out, is a kind of test case and proving ground not only for so-called vocational jobs but for how most *any* livelihood can be understood as a vocation in the fullest sense of the term. When we grasp why working with your hands—a practice looked down on by the world from time out of mind—is worthy of praise and pleasing to God, then we can appreciate how all good work, however humble, can be an antidote to quiet desperation and an expression of the quiet ambition.

So let's get after it. How is it that manual labor can have spiritual value? And why does that matter for each of us, whether we wear a blue collar or a white one? What can we all learn from God's regard for the work of "the boobies of Birmingham"?

Embodied Creatures

Let it be said at the outset that the most fundamental reason we can say that working with your hands is good is because God has made us as creatures who *have* hands—which is to say, we are *embodied*. We are neither mere hunks of flesh nor willowy spirits; we are the unique body-and-soul conglomeration that God calls humans. And what's more, he deems such creatureliness good, and very good.

So God made us to be embodied creatures. What, then, are we to *do* with these bodies? Taking our cue from the creation story, it's clear that fundamental to our very sense of personhood is working with our hands. Genesis 2:15 says, "The Lord God took the man and put him in the garden of Eden to work it and keep it." Our first human father isn't laid back sipping piña coladas and watching Netflix. He's down in the dirt, tilling, sowing, tending.

To be sure, work—including manual labor—isn't always a joy. Especially for those who work with their bodies, "the hand must ache, the face must sweat."[7] It can be toil! But it's theologically significant that the summons to labor occurs, so to speak, "pre-Fall." Work, in other words, was not a stopgap instituted by God after sin entered the world, much less a punishment. It was part of his original good intention for creation. Only once the rift opened up between him and his creatures does it become the case for Adam and Adam's seed that the ground is "cursed" and that "in pain you shall eat of it all the days of your life; thorns and thistles it shall bring forth for you; and you shall eat the plants of the field. By the sweat of your face you shall eat bread, till you return to the ground" (Gen 3:17-19). In the beginning it was not so, and still in this mortal life there can be tastes of work not cursed.

We get a feel for the goodness of working as creatures with bodies in Leo Tolstoy's classic *Anna Karenina*. In the novel, Constantine Dmitrich Levin is a wealthy landowner in nineteenth-century Russia. As a gentleman he is able to exempt himself from manual labor, practically by definition. But when his more cosmopolitan brother, Sergius, visits from the city, Levin grows weary of their overly intellectual conversations; he longs to engage his body. And so a novel idea dawns on him: to join his cadre of peasants by taking up the scythe and helping to mow his vast estate.

At first, Levin is self-conscious and worried he'll look foolish before his help. As the work continues, though, he feels the sweet pleasure of applying his body to the task at hand. "The perspiration in which he was bathed was cooling, and the sun which burnt his back, his head and his arm—bare to the elbow—added to his strength and perseverance in his task, and those unconscious intervals when it became possible not to think of what he was doing recurred more and more often. The scythe seemed to mow of itself. Those were happy moments."

As he goes on, pushing through his pain—which, drawing attention to muscles long neglected, itself isn't altogether unwelcome—the joy of Levin's work seems to escalate to a more spiritual state: not just happy but *blessed.*

> The longer Levin went on mowing, the oftener he experienced those moments of oblivion when his arms no longer seemed to swing the scythe, but the scythe itself his whole body, so conscious and full of life; and as if by magic, regularly and definitely without a thought being given to it, the work accomplished itself of its own accord. *These were blessed moments.*[8]

You have probably had moments like this. Times when you're pounding nails, patching clothes, or—like Levin—mowing the lawn, and suddenly the tick-tock of the clock evaporates. Athletes of every skill level know the sensation well. You get into that flow state and experience the pure pleasure of embodied motion.

Working with our hands is good because God made us as embodied creatures, and when we labor and play in ways that engage these bodies it affirms and celebrates his creation. And not only that, it serves our fellow creatures. We've skirted around it to this point, but here we run full up to the Christian teaching of vocation.

God's Masks

The term *vocation* has mixed connotations. Growing up at your typical white-bread, middle-class, suburban high school, my alma mater had so-called vocational programs. These were the ones prepping students for careers in the trades: welding, carpentry, auto repair—that sort of thing. I suspect this continues to be the association that most people have with the word, though that may be changing.[9] Here I want to suggest that the designation was right, but for the wrong reasons.

Many of my peers and I looked down on the "vocational" students. They were regarded as not as smart, and—since many of them came from working-class families whose parents were themselves blue-collar workers—there was undoubtedly a class distinction as well. By contrast, the rest of us were on track for college and interesting careers in "knowledge work," creative endeavors, business—white collars. This bias only ramped up among my friends at college, especially the ministry-minded among us. We were going to pursue our passions and follow our True Callings.[10]

You can see how the mythology was (and is) constructed. While in a sense I shared the latter path with my peers, I can no longer share its negative assessment of the "vocational" kids. Nor is my change of heart simply a matter of knowing that many of my fellow students who pursued the path of the trades didn't fit the stereotype, though that is certainly the case. More fundamentally, the problem is a category mistake: it's not vocation *versus* calling; it's vocation *as* calling.

The word comes from the Latin verb *vocare*, "to call." The implication is that God is the one who is on the other end of the line, so to speak. Scripture speaks of God calling in different senses: (1) he calls all people to faith and trust in him (Rom 1:6; 1 Cor 1:9); (2) he calls those who trust in him to a life of discipleship (Mt 4:18-22); (3) he calls his disciples to various and sundry occupations and estates where they are able to live out their faith (1 Cor 7:17-23); and (4) he calls some disciples to a particular office in service to his church (Eph 4:11-12).

One of the principal insights of the sixteenth-century Reformation was that the medieval church had collapsed the third and fourth sense of "calling" into a single category. Only those who served, as we might say today, in full-time "church work" had a genuine calling, *a vocation*. In a very real sense, other "worldly" occupations simply existed to help resource the important, *spiritual* callings of priest, monastic, and (later) missionary. Recovering the significance of the priesthood of all believers, the reformers insisted that God is at work in *all* sectors of society, and all Christians—whatever their trade or occupation—truly have a calling, a *vocation* from God.[11]

Martin Luther used a felicitous phrase that encapsulates this doctrine of vocation: "masks of God." He wrote,

> God could easily give you grain and fruit without your plowing and planting. But He does not want to do so. . . . What else is all our work to God—whether in the fields, in the garden, in the city, in the house, in war, or in government—but just such a child's performance, by which He wants to give His gifts in the fields, at home, and everywhere else? *These are the masks of God, behind which He wants to remain concealed and do all things.*
>
> We have the saying: "God gives every good thing, but not just by waving a hand." God gives all good gifts; but you must lend a hand and take the bull by the horns.
>
> Make the bars and gates, and let Him fasten them. Labor, and let Him give the fruits. Govern, and let Him give His blessing. Fight, and let Him give the victory. Preach, and let Him win hearts. Take a husband or a wife, and let Him produce the children. Eat and drink, and let Him nourish and strengthen you. And so on. *In all our doings He is to work through us, and He alone shall have the glory from it.*[12]

Thus, God can and does "conceal" himself under the guise of those who work with their hands, even as he conceals himself under the bread and wine of the Eucharist. Whether you are a butcher, a baker, or a candlestick maker, you can be doing good and godly labor. What matters more than the circumstances of the work—whether it's a woodshop, assembly line, or cubicle—is the faith of the worker.

While most Christians today would undoubtedly echoes Luther's insights in theory, in practice all too often we still live this sort of stratification. A friend of mine served on the board of a Christian liberal arts college that also has a long history of educating future pastors, youth ministers, teachers in Christian schools, and the like. In one meeting members of the board were wringing their hands about the continued decline in the number of church workers. Yes, enrollment overall was growing, and more and more future nurses, coaches, engineers, and others received a top-flight education from a confessing Christian college. But if they weren't raising up more pastors, wasn't the institution ultimately failing in its mission?

My friend, who served for a number of years as a missionary in the mountains of the Philippines, sat back and took in the conversation for some time. Finally, after a sufficient amount of weeping and gnashing of teeth, he spoke up. "We're lamenting the loss of full-time church workers, by which we mean those who are trained *by* the church to work *in* the church and be paid *by* the church—right?" Head nods around the table. "But what if instead we actually practiced what we preached about vocation and defined 'full-time church workers' not only as pastors and youth ministers but also as those who are trained by the church to work in the *world* and be paid by the world and bring God's light to the world—wherever they might be." The room got quiet for a moment before one of the other board members finally said, "Well, it looks like we've never had more full-time church workers coming through our school!" And the room burst out in cheers.

For believers, this is the life-affirming joy of vocation. Because you recognize that wherever and however you labor, it's good work—*holy* work—caught up and sanctified under the aegis of Christ and his Spirit. "The doctrine of vocation amounts to a comprehensive doctrine of the Christian life," Gene Edward Veith writes, "having to do with faith and sanctification, grace and good works. . . . It shows how Christians can influence their culture. It transfigures ordinary, everyday life with the presence of God."[13]

Helping People Out

What Luther emphasized most of all about vocation is that we work well when we work for others. As we said in chapter six, God doesn't need your good works—or your good *work*—but your neighbor does. And to be clear, you can and do accomplish this in all manner of white-collar professions as well; I'm certainly not trying to introduce a new gradation of holy occupations that just flips the old on its head. Rather, it's a straightforward recognition that manual work is often more immediately beneficial to your neighbor.

I've been struck by an admonition of Saint Paul in Ephesians. He gets to the point in the letter where he is providing moral instruction and exhortation, having laid a foundation of salvation by grace, when he says this: "Let the thief no longer steal, but rather let him labor, doing honest work with his own hands, so that he may have something to share with anyone in need" (Eph 4:28). It's like he's saying, "Listen, you want to reverse your no-good grifting ways? Build something, fix something, knit something, because making's the opposite of taking."[14]

Sometimes when I get around a table with friends I like to ask the question, "What would you like to do for work if you weren't doing what you're doing?" I find it to be an illuminating question to get into the personality of people: What are their longings, what do they enjoy but also feel they're missing? Almost invariably the answers are some kind of work with your hands, something more tangible: painting or carpentry or barbering. Once, my wife surprised the group by answering, "Midwife." Raised eyebrows and surprised looks asked, *Really?* "Yeah," she said with a smile, "because midwives help people out."

Which reminds me of perhaps my favorite story of quiet ambition in the Old Testament. At the beginning of Exodus, we meet the anonymous new pharaoh of Egypt who is like the conniving, large-headed rat of the nineties cartoon *Pinky and the Brain*: he wants to try and take over the world. Recognizing how the exponential growth of the Israelites may provide an obstacle to his aspirations, he makes a diabolical decree: "Then the king of Egypt said to the Hebrew midwives, one of whom was named Shiphrah and the other Puah, 'When you serve as midwife to the Hebrew women and see them on the birthstool, if it is a son, you shall kill him, but if it is a daughter, she shall live'" (Ex 1:15-16). The reader is horrified by the command. And what could a pair of lowly old midwives do in the face of such grave evil?

> But the midwives feared God and did not do as the king of Egypt commanded them, but let the male children live. So the king of Egypt called the midwives and said to them, "Why have you done this, and let the male children live?" The midwives said to Pharaoh, "Because the Hebrew women are not like the Egyptian women, for they are vigorous and give birth before the midwife comes to them." So God dealt well with the midwives. (Ex 1:17-20)

In short, midwives help people out.

And, of course, once the babies are out, the dirty jobs don't stop. As the father of four whose youngest was potty trained but a few years ago, I remember it all too well. But as Luther reminds us, that simply means more opportunities for practicing largeness in littleness. "God, with all his angels and creatures," the Reformer writes, "smiles when the Christian father is washing diapers, because he is doing so in faith."[15]

Working with our hands is good because God hides himself behind the masks of his human creatures. But sometimes, his presence in manual labor hasn't been so hidden.

Who's Who in the Bible

The annual *Time* list of most influential people is an instructive reflection of the age in which we live. The list nowadays is commonly populated with tech wizards and entrepreneurs, politicians and celebrities. Then there is the nebulous category of "influencer" and the dubious vocation of "YouTuber." These are the kinds of careers that society tends to revere and emulate, and many have enviable qualities. Suffice it to say, however, that—save for the stray athlete like Patrick Mahomes—these aren't folks who work with their hands. Nary a farmer or carpenter among them.

Contrast that with the biblical record—to be sure, there's an element of anachronism here; "knowledge workers" wasn't a category in the ancient world. When you start to list manual laborers in the Bible, it's practically a who's who of Scripture. There's Noah the shipbuilder, Ruth the gleaner, and Nehemiah the cupbearer-turned-mason. Famously, several of the apostles are fishermen by trade: Andrew and Peter, James and John. And then there's Saul-turned-Paul, the original worker-priest, who subsidized his ministry with a tentmaker gig on the side. Not to mention the prodigious number of shepherds: Moses, David, Amos. And most of all the Good Shepherd, our Lord Jesus.

And Jesus' familiarity with working with his hands goes further. At one point in the Gospel of Mark, as Jesus went about in his hometown of Nazareth teaching, the befuddled crowd cries out, "Where did this man get these things? What is the wisdom given to him? How are such mighty works done by his hands? *Is not this the carpenter?*" (Mk 6:2-3, emphasis added).

The Greek word translated "carpenter" here is *tektōn*, the root of our English word "architect" (or "chief builder"; cf. 1 Cor 3:10). A *tektōn* was commonly one who worked in wood and stone. The word is used in the Septuagint (the Greek translation of the Old Testament) to denote Israelite blacksmiths (1 Sam 3:19), King Hiram's craftsmen who built David's house (2 Sam 5:11), and the variety of workmen Solomon employed to erect the temple (1 Chron 22:15). In sum, a *tektōn* knew his way around the shop.

The astonished crowds of Jesus' day, who were well acquainted with "Joseph & Son Construction," are therefore asking in effect, "How can this guy who merely works with his hands do such works . . . *with his hands?*" Though they lacked Tesla and Meta, they did not want for "influencers"—and to a person, you could be certain such people did not come from the ranks of manual laborers. "Manual labor was despised by ancient Greek culture," notes biblical commentator David Guzik. "They thought that the better a man was, the less he should work. In contrast, God gave us a carpenter King, fisherman apostles, and tent-making missionaries."[16]

Working with our hands is thus good and God-pleasing because it follows in the footsteps of our Lord Jesus. And in the Lord's own adoption of the quiet ambition we behold the scope and means of the redemption that he effects. Tish Harrison Warren, in her book *The Liturgy of the Ordinary*, beautifully reflects on the significance of Jesus' own ordinariness:

> Christ's ordinary years are part of our redemption story. Because of the incarnation and those long, unrecorded years of Jesus' life, our small, normal lives matter. If Christ was a carpenter, all of us who are in Christ find that our work is sanctified and made holy. If Christ spent time in obscurity, then there is infinite worth found in obscurity. If Christ spent most of his life in quotidian ways, then all of life is brought under his lordship. There is no task too small or too routine to reflect God's glory and worth.[17]

In Christ, then, all work takes on a different cast. As Saint Paul writes in Colossians, "And whatever you do, in word or deed, do everything in the name of the Lord Jesus" (3:17). The name of the Lord, applied to you in baptism, transforms your identity and work, making it ever and always an opportunity to serve.

Polishing Forks for the Kingdom

In the critically acclaimed television show *The Bear*, Richie is a middle-aged divorcé who is worn out from slinging sandwiches at the family diner. In one episode (titled "Forks"), his brother's best friend and boss, Carmen, sends him away to help out at a primo restaurant at which Carmen himself used to be a chef.[18] But Richie doesn't get to prepare appetizing entrees or even wait tables, at least not at first. He has to polish forks . . . by hand. For hour after tedious hour, he toils to clean streaks from flatware. It's manual labor at its most menial.

At his lowest point, Richie is utterly fed up and ready for someone to stick a fork in him. His (much younger) supervisor, Garrett, lets him know some of his forks still aren't properly cleaned. "I've been doing this for nine hours," Richie says. "I think I know what's clean." Garrett persists. "Yo, they're %&$# forks!" Richie says—to which Garrett summarily summons him outside.

"Do you think this work is below you?" Garrett asks. "Man, I think I'm forty-five years old polishing forks," Richie says. Garrett sighs and then launches into a speech that starts to turn the tide for Richie. "We have a waiting list that is five thousand people long," Garrett says. "People wait in line to spend their hard-earned time and money here. I'm sorry, bro, but we need to give them some forks without streaks in them. Every day here is the freaking Super Bowl."

Richie starts to see that it's not about the forks; it's about the people who use them. At one point, granted a reprieve from polishing duty, he is called on to serve a table with a surprise treat. He sees his sparkling silverware put to use in conveying a delectable delight into the waiting mouths of guests. In that moment, he's given a glimpse of how his little labor fits into the grand scheme of things. As another chef tells him, "Every night we get to make someone's day."

Richie has arrived at his own fork: Will he look at his labor—even the tedious, polishing-forks-by-hand labor—as meaningless toil or as a meaningful vocation? The key, he realizes, is seeing it as an occasion to help people out, as an opportunity to *serve*.

How much more is this true for us who know that we are not just employees in an earthly enterprise but subjects of the King of kings? And yet at times we too find ourselves at that fork, whether our livelihood is manual labor or knowledge work: blue collar, white collar, clerical collar—or no collar at all.

At the end of the day, we're all polishing forks for the kingdom. Some days it can seem mind-numbingly tedious and meaningless. But some days we get a glimpse that we are preparing for the marriage feast of the Lamb in his kingdom that is without end, when no longer will our bread come from the sweat of our face, when every day will be bigger and better than the freaking Super Bowl.

8

THE NEED TO KNEAD

WHEN I SAW THE PRINT ON ETSY, I realized that I had overlooked a key part of 1 Thessalonians 4:11.

If you're unfamiliar with the website, Etsy is "the global marketplace for unique and creative goods."[1] Replete with arts and crafts products, it's akin to a more artisanal, online version of Hobby Lobby. And like Hobby Lobby, it's not uncommon to find stuff with Scripture verses plastered on it—such as the print in question.

This particular one was of a sort you often see these days: printed on a rectangular, cream-colored canvas, with a faux-wood frame around it, in cursive script were written the words "Make it your ambition to lead a quiet life." Then below this line, in all-caps, were the words "AND WORK WITH YOUR HANDS." And that's when it struck me that there is more to this little phrase than first meets the eye.

Given the context, the Etsy print (which, I'll admit, now hangs over my hearth) was presumably extolling not manual labor but something else, something more native to its habitat. What dawned on me was that not only roofers and lumberjacks work with their hands; so, too, do people who enjoy pottery or whittling or arts and crafts of all kinds. Even if Saint Paul didn't have scrapbooking in mind when he encouraged the Thessalonians to work with their hands, we intuitively understand that his words have resonance with an elemental aspect of our humanity, one that is consistently affirmed in the Scriptures: the capacity to be *creative*.

Perhaps it's fitting that, as creatures with two hands, there should be two ways of talking about what it means to work with them. The *Oxford English Dictionary* makes the intuition explicit: to work with one's hands not only can have the sense "to be employed in a manual job or trade"; it can also mean "to make something by hand."[2] The definition of the related term "handiwork" teases this out even further: it is "the product of the manual or creative labor of a person."[3]

So on the one hand (if you will pardon the pun), working with your hands can mean polishing forks and plumbing toilets, changing diapers and doing dishes. But on the other hand, it can mean creative endeavors—exercising that part of your created nature that delights in making stuff, imagining worlds, solving problems, whether in your vocations or avocations, your livelihood or your leisure pursuits. In short, working with your hands is a matter not only of manual labor but also of labors of love.

In this chapter I wish to explore this second "hand-sense": the impulse toward creativity. First, we will reflect on the creative calling (and whether it applies to us all). Then, we'll look at the contemporary conditions that tempt us to surrender the calling. And finally, we'll consider one particular creative pastime that provides both an entry point for working with your hands and an analogy that shows in what ways handiwork helps to quell quiet desperation.

The Creative Calling

I don't usually go looking for theological wisdom from record producers, but then again Rick Rubin isn't just any record producer. The man in the studio behind legendary musical acts like the Beastie Boys, Johnny Cash, Metallica, the Avett Brothers, and many more, Rubin truly is "the guy behind the guy." He also has a hairdo that makes him look vaguely like a Muppets character, which is a plus.

Rubin's bestselling book *The Creative Act* is a fascinating and at times even enlightening read. His spiritual insights are often unorthodox, to be sure, and wouldn't pass muster with many doctrinal review boards. But having worked with countless artists of various kinds, he has a keen understanding of creativity that Christians would do well to heed.

"You exist as a creative being in a creative universe," Rubin writes. "A singular work of art."[4] He has hit the nail on the head—or, should we say, he has struck the right note. But Rubin doesn't ask what I consider to be the natural next question: Where does that creativity come from?

The creative calling is present from the very beginning of time. In words that echo through the ages, God intones, "Let us make man in our image, after our likeness." Then Moses reports, "So God created man in his own image, in the image of God he created him; male and female he created them" (Gen 1:26-27). Humans are thus made "in the image of God."

Untold amounts of ink have been spilled over this concept of the *imago Dei*. Customarily when we think of what it means to be made in God's likeness, what comes to mind are features like our human capacity for reasoning, perhaps, or memory or language—all of which are true and essential to our image-of-God-ness. But there's still more.

The most salient feature of God's likeness that is reflected in the beginning is precisely his creativity. Consider how we name him in the first article of the Apostles' Creed: "I believe in God, the Father Almighty, *maker* of heaven and earth." The Psalms often speak of this, perhaps most famously in Psalm 19: "The heavens declare the glory of God, and the sky above proclaims his *handiwork*" (emphasis added). Or Psalm 95: "For the Lord is a great God, and a great King above all gods. In his hand are the depths of the earth; the heights of the mountains are his also. The sea is his, for he made it, and his hands formed the dry land" (Ps 95:3-5).

The book of Job beautifully expresses the creative nature of God. For instance, when the long-suffering man is questioned by the Lord about his work of creation:

> Where were you when I laid the foundation of the earth?
> Tell me, if you have understanding.
> Who determined its measurements—surely you know!
> Or who stretched the line upon it?
> On what were its bases sunk,
> or who laid its cornerstone,
> when the morning stars sang together
> and all the sons of God shouted for joy? (Job 38:4-7)

God's heart for creativity is also reflected in early Israel. In chapter seven we looked at the biblical who's who of people who were, to varying degrees, tradesmen and manual laborers. One notable character left off that list you may not recognize by name, but he had an outsized role in biblical history: Bezalel, son of Uri. Bezalel is the first person in the Bible to be described as filled with the Spirit. What's especially remarkable about this is that he is neither a prophet nor a priest, much less a king. No, Bezalel is a craftsman:

> See, I have called by name Bezalel the son of Uri, son of Hur, of the tribe of Judah, and I have filled him with the Spirit of God, with ability and intelligence, with knowledge and all craftsmanship, to devise artistic designs, to work in gold, silver, and bronze, in cutting stones for setting, and in carving wood, to work in every craft. (Ex 31:2-5)

Bezalel (along with his right-hand man, Oholiab, the son of Ahisamach) is no mere handyman. He's an artist, called and equipped by God to spearhead the erection of the tabernacle, the Lord's dwelling place with humankind, and its furnishings. The example of Bezalel is a stirring affirmation of the creative calling and the godly potential for working with your hands.

Time would fail us to tell of the countless believers through the ages who have faithfully reflected the heart of God through their creative labors: the cathedrals constructed by myriad anonymous saints, the icons of Rublev, the dramas of Dickens, the cantatas of that musical evangelist Johann Sebastian Bach, who offered up the works of his hands unto the Lord, signing them S.D.G.—*soli Deo gloria*, "To God alone be the glory."

Ours is a God for whom creativity is at the heart of his very being. Whoever else God is for us, he is undeniably also the divine artist, the agent of cosmic creativity.[5]

This is the God in whose image you have been made. Your very essence reflects a Creator who not only delights in the work of his hands—the *product* of his creativity—but also, if we can put it this way, the very task of working with his divine hands—the *process* of creativity. You can't read Job, for instance, without getting the impression that God really enjoys this stuff. So it shouldn't come as a surprise when we, as his human creatures, also enjoy working with our hands and being creative.

You may have a creative vocation for your livelihood. But even if you work with your hands as an avocation, that doesn't make it frivolous, not by a long shot. It's an elemental expression of the *imago Dei* within you. "We are [God's] workmanship," Paul writes in Ephesians, "created in Christ Jesus for good works" (Eph 2:10). We are labors of love, laboring in love.

Creative All

But what if you don't deem yourself to be "creative"? Maybe you hear this talk about creativity and think, *That's great for Bach and Caravaggio, but I'm not a card-carrying member of the creative class. I'm just a regular, uncreative Joe.*

If our view of creativity is limited to the imaginative person who is making new works of art—the painter in her studio, the pianist at the keys—then sure, we don't all fit that mold. But when we grasp that creativity is part of our nature as people made in the image of God, then we can start to see the manifold means by which we're *all* creative—in ways we may never have even realized.

In his book *Living into Focus*, author Arthur Boers (whom I mentioned briefly in chapter three) interviews a variety of people with pastimes that involve working with their hands: things like quilting, letter writing, woodworking, and more. Drawing on the work of philosopher Albert Borgmann, Boers dubs these creative outlets *focal practices*: "activities that center, balance, focus, and orient one's life."[6]

Boers relates how, in the course of his interviews, he was struck by the fact that most of these folks were surprised that he even wanted to talk with them. After all, they didn't think of themselves as "creative." They were even a little reticent at first to discuss something that they feared others might regard as just a quirky hobby ("Who writes letters anymore?"). But once he gave them permission, as it were, to discuss their devotion to gardening or knack for knitting, he could hardly get them to stop talking. People are passionate about their creative endeavors, even if they don't always recognize them as such.

I've seen this time and again in congregations, especially among folks who have more "professional" jobs. They may answer phones at the dentist's office or adjust insurance claims to make a living, but they live for crocheting caps for their grandchildren or carving figurines out of a little block of basswood . . . just because.

I think of Caleb, a quiet, thoughtful doctor. I was visiting with him at his home, and in the course of our conversation he related how his work in medicine had grown increasingly to feel like an administrative job in which he simply shuffled a lot of paperwork. I asked him what he liked to do in his free time. With a sheepish grin, he took me to his garage. There he showed me the old roadster he loved monkeying around on with his boys. There was no clear path to making the car roadworthy anytime soon, but he delighted in the creative problem solving required under the hood.

My mind returns to that thoughtful producer, Rick Rubin. "Creativity is not a rare ability," he writes. "It is not difficult to access. Creativity is a fundamental aspect of being human. It's our birthright. And it's for all of us. Creativity doesn't exclusively relate to making art. We all engage in this act on a daily basis." He goes on:

> To create is to bring something into existence that wasn't there before. It could be a conversation, the solution to a problem, a note to a friend, the rearrangement of furniture in a room, a new route home to avoid a traffic jam. What you make doesn't have to be witnessed, recorded, sold, or encased in glass for it to be a work of art.[7]

The creative impulse is latent in us all. You don't have to be an artist or musician to exercise it. You do, however, need to beware the temptation in our modern world to *surrender* it.

Life Aboard the Axiom

Wouldn't it be great if you could have whatever you want, whenever you want it, without needing to gain it or make it by the work of your own hands? Pixar's prescient 2008 film *WALL-E* raises this question and responds in compelling fashion.[8]

The movie portrays a world in the not-too-distant future that is supposed to be utopia. Humans have taken up residence aboard the outer-space cruise ship the *Axiom* (funded by retail mega-giant "Buy-n-Large"), in which your every wish is granted at the touch of a button—while you continue to recline atop your hovering armchair. A pleasant voice intones over the PA, "Buy-n-Large: everything you need to be happy!" Lunch-in-a-cup is delivered directly to your hover-chair. Screens projected inches in front of the passive viewers constantly pipe in prepackaged entertainment (alongside a steady stream of ads, of course). Liberated from labor, people swell up to comic proportions; the population looks like a band of oversized babies. Consumption has wholly supplanted creation.

Would it be great to live in a world where you are freed from the need to work with your hands? The movie answers with a resounding *no*: life aboard the *Axiom* looks a lot more like a dystopia. It takes a spunky little garbage-collecting robot called WALL-E to help recover a more human future for the erstwhile occupants of earth. And tellingly, essential to the rescue strategy is reconnecting with creation: WALL-E has to deliver a fragile seedling, a sign of life from a forgotten planet, into the heart of the *Axiom* in order to initiate the return voyage home. The movie concludes with the bewildered humans putting the precious young plant into the ground as the captain of the ship explains, "This is called farming!" The epilogue during the end credits shows people creating anew: gardening and building and painting and more. It's a beautiful coda to a moving film—one that helps us understand just what is at issue in our adoption (or lack thereof) of the quiet ambition's calling to work with our hands.

The problem is not that some of us are creative and that some of us are not. The problem, as *WALL-E* so powerfully portrays, is that our consumerist digital age seduces us to surrender our creative nature for a life of passive consumption.

Master craftsman Doug Stowe agrees. In his book *The Wisdom of Our Hands*, Stowe marvels at the diverse expressions and benefits of creative handiwork. "The hands have been the fundamental means through which the world has been shaped, measured, studied, and understood," he writes. He observes how the hand itself is a tool—used for kneading, grasping, cutting, striking, and so on—and how all the actions of tools come from the motions of human hands.

"Our hands are the means by which we test the substance of the physical world and come to an understanding of our place within it," Stowe writes. "With our hands, we measure the temperature, the weight, and the shape of things and whether they are coarse or smooth. So, the hands are not only instruments of creativity; they are also sensing devices without which our understanding of our world would be incomplete."[9] Coining a delightful phrase, Stowe praises the blessings of "sawdust therapy."

For this reason, Stowe laments the state of our present world, in which we are increasingly disconnected from the work of our hands. "Either we are active participants in the creation of human culture, or we are passive consumers of it," he writes. "Those who make things—whether lovely, handcrafted things from wood, or music, or spaghetti—have a leg up on, or should I say a stronger grasp than, those who allow themselves to become idle consumers of a culture produced by others."[10]

Wendell Berry trenchantly underscores this point in his classic essay "The Pleasures of Eating." He observes how specialization of production has led to specialization of consumption, so that now "patrons of the entertainment industry, for example, entertain themselves less and less and have become more and more passively dependent on commercial suppliers." True to his core concerns, Berry then turns to the food industry, whose patrons have "tended more and more to be mere consumers." With wry fatalism, Berry concludes: "The ideal industrial food consumer would be strapped to a table with a tube running from the food factory directly into his or her stomach."[11] He might as well be describing the passengers aboard the *Axiom*. We're all tempted to live on it now: a hurtling spaceship of hopelessness.

But it doesn't have to be this way. Consumption has its place, and there is no sin in enjoying the works of others' creativity (such as *WALL-E!*). We are, however, created to be creative; to work with our hands as an expression of God's image within us and for the benefit of our neighbors. This aspect of the quiet ambition is available to us all. So what's an easy entry point for being more creative? And moreover, what is it about creativity that pushes back on the dread effects of quiet desperation?

An answer to these questions can be found in the baking supplies aisle of your local market—though for a moment, it couldn't.

The Need to Knead

Amid the dreary days of pandemic lockdowns, a surprising product began disappearing from grocery store shelves. No, not toilet paper. (That wasn't especially surprising). I speak of yeast, one of the essential ingredients for baking bread.[12] An unexpected byproduct of the pandemic, it seems, was a resurgence of home bakers.

Alas, the boom was short-lived; already by 2021 there were 195 million fewer home-baked goods (including a sharp 28 percent decline in homemade bread), which dipped even below prepandemic levels.[13] At least you won't have any trouble picking up a jar of yeast from the market—and I'd like to encourage you to do so, especially if you're seeking a starting point for incorporating more "handcraft" into your everyday life. Baking bread serves well as both example of and metaphor for the value of working with your hands.

To begin with, baking bread is the consummate example of a creative outlet for the quiet ambition because it's simple, it's slow, and it's scriptural. First, it's simple. Bread requires only four ingredients, which are inexpensive and (pandemic conditions aside) easy to come by: flour, water, and salt, as well as yeast. You need no fancy tools, especially if you knead by hand. A basic kitchen oven will suffice for the baking itself. More than anything, bread just takes time—which points to the second reason I commend it to you.

Baking bread does take time. It is inherently a slow process. "Instant yeast" notwithstanding, you can't eliminate the period of fermentation in which the dough is rising and the flavor is forming. Crucially, this process itself is essential to the final product; as baker and author Peter Reinhart observes, "Fermentation is the single most important stage in the creation of great bread."[14] Like the gestation of a baby or the percolation of a pot of coffee, fermentation just takes the time it takes.[15] Quiet desperation is sped along by the acceleration of modern life; in contrast, the dough's slow rise is part and parcel with the quiet ambition.

Third, I would be remiss not to mention the rich scriptural resonance of bread. As we pray in the Lord's Prayer, bread is the epitome of God's daily provision of our creaturely needs (Mt 6:11; cf. Ps 104:15). Bread recalls his miraculous care for Israel in the wilderness (Ex 16), even as we recognize that bread alone cannot supplant his word (Deut 8:3; Lk 4:4). Finally, in the Eucharist bread becomes the supernatural vehicle of Christ's sacramental presence (1 Cor 10:16)—he who himself professed to be "the Bread of Life" (Jn 6:48). In short, the humble art of baking bread connects us to the exalted horizons of transcendent truth.

So if you are looking for a simple starting point for folding in more creativity into your everyday life, I encourage you to make a visit to the baking aisle at your local market. Baking bread is easy to do, facilitates a salutary slowdown, and roots you in the biblical narrative. Not to mention it's delicious, and your family and friends will thank you!

Baking bread is not only a method for working with your hands, however; it's also a metaphor that illuminates the curative powers of creativity more generally.

Consider the process of baking bread at its most elemental level.[16] You start with flour, which is essentially dead and pulverized grain (usually wheat). The flour is mixed with water and salt to make a lifeless lump of clay. Then, you inject *leaven* (such as yeast), a word that literally means "to raise up." That lump of clay is now a living organism: your labor breathes into it the breath of life, bringing forth into the world something that before did not exist. And then, with time and heat, that vital ball of dough will be transformed—glorified, you might say—in order to create the gratuitous, delectable gift of bread.

The metaphysical drama unfolding in this process is unmistakable. While some of its features are unique to bread baking, the general contours are commensurate with most any expression of creative handiwork. In creativity, as J. R. R. Tolkien suggested in his seminal essay "On Fairy-Stories," we act as "sub-creators."[17] Only God creates *ex nihilo*, out of nothing, but we enter into his labor when we work with our hands, whether the fruit of our creativity is a sourdough loaf, an entertaining story, or a purring engine.

Another benefit of creating is that it asserts what psychologists call the sense of personal agency. Quiet desperation saps your hope by sucking your purpose; it sets in when we feel as though our little lives fail to make a mark on the world. Creative labor, then, stands as an objective refutation to the claim it's all in vain. (Interestingly, an optional latter stage of the bread-baking process is known as "proofing.") Like the proud Chuck Noland (Tom Hanks) in *Cast Away* after he successfully puts his hands to making that most elemental of creations—fire—we also can stand back with an awed and grateful sense of accomplishment: "I have baked this loaf! I have built this shelf!"

And last but certainly not least, the blessed gratuitousness of creativity is not to be neglected. Though we pray that our Father would "give us this day our daily bread," strictly speaking we can subsist on less glorious fodder; many humans have and do. But a beautiful and tasty loaf of bread, like all creative handiwork, is an affirmation of the inherent wonder and goodness of being alive. The sheer fact of created existence is grace, and creativity taps into that reality. As Martin Luther writes in his Small Catechism on the first article of the Apostles' Creed, "I believe that God has made me together with all creatures . . . and all this He has done out of His divine, fatherly goodness and mercy, without any merit or worthiness in me." Bread says, it's all good.

We all have the need to knead. We all have been made in the image of the Almighty Maker, endowed with the urge to create. For you it might not be in the kitchen but instead at the sewing machine, in the shop, or outside in the garden. In whatever way or place our creativity takes shape, the key is to resist the all-consuming draw of the *Axiom* and to embrace our identity as sub-creators who can offer up the works of our hands, however small, to the glory of God, as I learned firsthand from Lance.

Soli Deo Gloria

When I first met Lance, I wouldn't have taken him for the creative type. I don't think he would have taken *himself* for that. He has more the persona of a dude rancher. He stands 6'3" with a handlebar mustache and a laugh that can be heard two states away. He wears cross-shaped pins that are draped in the flag, often sports a black ball cap that has on it a rifle and 2A, and whenever his phone rings he gets a greeting from (as he refers to him) "45." He also has the kindest heart you can imagine.

Once upon a time, Lance had designs on ministry. Sure of his path, he and his wife, Caroline, pulled up stakes and moved across the country to attend seminary. But he's a right-brain thinker, and the left-brain exactitude needed to learn Greek, the language of the New Testament, quickly did him in. After only a few months, Lance dropped out.

Head hung low, he and Caroline retreated to their hometown to pick up the pieces. Hadn't God called him? Didn't he have good works prepared for him? It was a real moment of vocational and even existential crisis. But existential crises have to wait when you've just got to find a way to put food on the table, and after spending their savings to make the move to seminary, Lance had to find work fast. One thing he knew he could do was work with his hands. He couldn't be a pastor, but at least he could be a painter.

Lance threw himself into the work and established a reputation in the community as not merely some utilitarian house painter but a real artist. He took pride in his work, doing it "as for the Lord and not for men." Still, he would speak wistfully of his missed opportunity for ministry, like a broken-hearted lover lamenting the one that got away. When a friend and fellow church member started seminary, you could hear the pious envy in Lance's voice when he asked about it. He relished in and excelled in his vocation as a painter, but it was nevertheless undeniable that he felt something was still missing.

And then one day Lance came to me with an idea. It had been excruciating for him, he said, to sit in our pews at church Sunday after Sunday. "Are my sermons really that bad?" I asked. He laughed. "No, it's not that," he said. "It's these walls. They're bare white and they have more cracks than Humpty Dumpty. Let me paint them." Then he laid out his vision for restoring the grandeur of our 140-year-old sanctuary. Frankly, I was a little skeptical, but I brought the plan to our church council, and a few months later Lance and his team began their work.

I could hardly believe the creative artistry. Not only was he able to restore nearly a half-mile of lineal feet of cracks in the aged plaster—no mean feat—but he brought back the historic stenciling, brought out the latent beauty of original architectural details, and all told made our house of God to look as good or better than when it was first built by German immigrants in the 1800s.

"Lance," I said, marveling, "you're a true artist." I wondered not only at the work done, but how God had worked in Lance's life. It hadn't gone how he had planned, but the Lord was undeniably using his creative gifts of "working with his hands" to bless many lives.

Lance tugged my sleeve. "There's one more thing I've got to show you," he said. He led me around to the entrance to the sanctuary. There, in dazzling gold letters over the doorway, were three words: *Soli Deo Gloria*.

When we work with our hands in a spirit of faith, we're not just making stuff. We're fashioning hope. We're leaning into the prayer of Moses in Psalm 90:17: "Let the favor of the Lord our God be upon us, and establish the work of our hands upon us; yes, establish the work of our hands!"

The Practice of Working with Your Hands

THE QUIET AMBITION IS a way that hope takes shape each day. Part of this path is to work with your hands, and in these chapters we explored two sides to this: on the one hand, the spiritual value of manual labor, and on the other hand, the God-given need to be creative. When we put these hands to work, in our vocations and avocations, we embrace our human creatureliness and ready ourselves for resurrected life.

Suggestions for practicing the quiet ambition

1. ***Ora et labora.*** The Benedictines' motto *ora et labora*, "pray and work," is a rhythm and a refrain for faithfully carrying out our vocations. Make it your own. The apostle Paul admonishes us, "Whatever you do, in word or deed, do everything in the name of the Lord Jesus" (Col 3:17). When we prayerfully labor, we do justice to the name of the Lord that we bear and find greater satisfaction in our work.

   - Take an inventory of your various vocations: son or daughter, spouse, parent, employee/employer, citizen, church member, etc. Journal about how you can "help people out" in each of those stations of life.
   - Singing sanctifies labor. Right before Colossians 3:17, we are encouraged to let the word of Christ dwell in us richly

"singing psalms and hymns and spiritual songs" (Col 3:16). Learn by heart some favorite hymns or praise songs, even Scripture set to music, and let them grace your lips as you do your work.

- Read John 13:1-15. Jesus washed feet; we can clean toilets. Take up this dirty job in a spirit of devotion and service, reflecting on your reading.

2. **Mow the lawn yourself.** I am all for supporting the local economy and helping young entrepreneurs who wish to make some spending money. Anymore, though, folks are farming out the yard work either because they are too busy or they find it too menial or both. Mow your own lawn, shovel your own driveway; recover the pure pleasure of moving your body. Better still: help out an aged neighbor by taking care of *their* yard or sidewalk, without comment, on the sly.
3. **Do a "digital declutter."** Our contemporary digital-age existence looks more like life aboard the *Axiom* each day. As embodied creatures designed for creation and not just consumption, it is vital that we exercise a healthy degree of asceticism toward technology and new media. In his book *Digital Minimalism*, Cal Newport recommends a digital declutter, "a reset for your digital life."[18] There are three steps:
   - Step 1: "Put aside a thirty-day period during which you will take a break from optional technologies in your life," such as apps, websites, and digital tools.
   - Step 2: "During this thirty-day break, explore and rediscover activities and behaviors that you find satisfying and meaningful." Replace passive consumption with active creation. Take up a new hobby. Spend more time with your kids.

- Step 3: "At the end of the break, reintroduce optional technologies into your life, starting from a blank slate." Only reintroduce those things that you deem genuinely valuable.

4. **Bake a fresh loaf for the potluck.** Baking bread is fun, and it's even more fun when it's baked to share. The next time you have a church potluck (and if your church doesn't have potlucks, what are you doing?), or when you're invited over to a friend's home for dinner, make your contribution the fresh-baked work of your hands. Don't feel compelled to churn your own butter, though, unless that's your jam (pun intended).

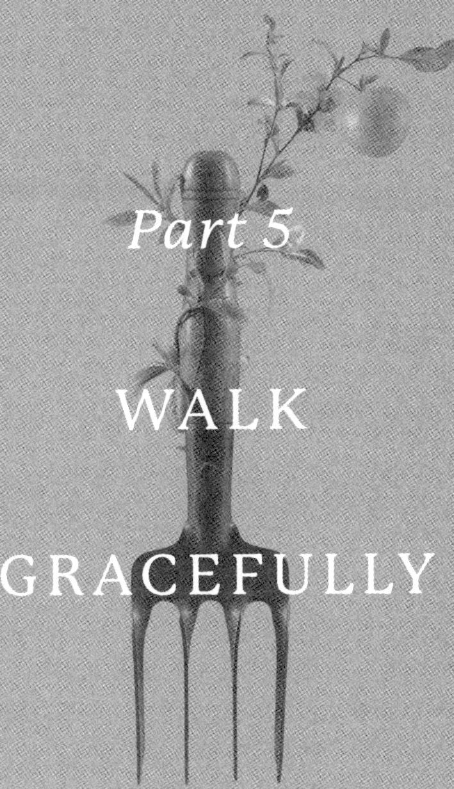

Part 5

WALK GRACEFULLY

9

MUSTARD SEED MISSIONARIES AND COFFEE BEAN CHRISTIANS

Our age has a burning ambition to "change the world." In his 2009 book *Culture Making*, Andy Crouch noted that 216 books in the Library of Congress had that specific phrase in their title. (Scintillating reads like *Mauve: The Color That Changed the World*.) What's even more interesting, though, is that a full third of those books had been published since 2000.[1]

Things have only ramped up in our society since the publication of Crouch's book. The Google Ngram viewer, which tracks the frequency with which words or phrases have been used in books (going back to 1800), helps to dramatically visualize the spike.

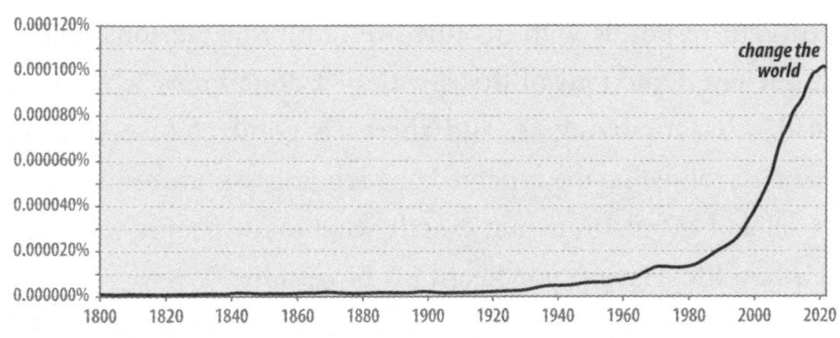

Figure 1. "Change the World" Ngram

Christians, too, can get caught up in the world-changing game. After all, God wants the gospel to reach all nations and intends nothing less than the renewal of all creation. If that's not world changing, what is? Shouldn't that always be the upshot of our lives as Christians? Many of us will be familiar with this message from pulpits, Sunday school classes, and youth group gatherings—and it isn't all wrong! But I wish to suggest that it has some serious flaws. It's high time we step back, take a deep breath, and give those world-changing aspirations closer consideration as we round the bend now to consider the upshot of quiet ambition.

What's the outcome of this way of living? Who does it ultimately serve? And how is it done? In this chapter we'll first consider the *what* and *how* questions, and in the next chapter the *who* and *why*.

As it turns out, the outcome of the unambitious ambition, as Paul tells it, is as modest as it is unexpected: "Make it your ambition to live quietly," he writes, "*so that you might walk gracefully toward outsiders*" (this is my own translation of a phrase commonly translated "behave properly"; more on this presently). In other words: the endgame of this seemingly very personal way of life is *witness*.

If this were being revised for a twenty-first-century audience, you can imagine Paul's PR crew trying to coach him. "Listen, Paul, people are all about self-help. How is this going to help them live their best life now, build a happier life, maximize their potential?" Then Paul responds with his furrowed unibrow (seriously, check out ancient depictions of the apostle), "I don't know what in the world self-actualizing is, and there's a good chance that any Christian following the crucified one is going to endure all manner of trial and tribulation—not exactly what many people would call their best life. Haven't you heard my biography?"

The aim of quiet ambition is therefore more honest, more modest, and more missional. While I'm sold on the fact that the biblical wisdom Paul encapsulates in these verses is a more hopeful alternative to the quiet disappointment that inevitably results from our restless, noisy age, that doesn't mean it's focused on merely personal growth or satisfaction. To the contrary, it remains engaged with the world. As biblical scholar Abraham Malherbe notes on this passage, "[Paul] did not advocate that his converts withdraw physically from society, but required a quality of life from the 'brothers' that was different from that of society."[2]

Quiet ambition has an eye toward witness and not simply self-help. But does this way of witness mean that we as Christians need to be about "changing the world"? If not, why not? And what could the alternative look like?

Why We Can't Change the World

There's a classic cartoon that has made its way around the internet over the years. A stick figure sits hunched over his computer, blank face transfixed on the screen, fingers feverishly tapping away. From the other room a voice calls: "Are you coming to bed?" The stick figure responds, "I can't. This is important." "What?" asks the voice. And our man at the computer says, "Someone is WRONG on the internet."

When as Christians we consider why we *can't* change the world, scale is a good place to start. Like a blogger futilely trying to "correct" the internet, the scope of the problem far exceeds the capacity of the actor.

But there are even more fundamental reasons for our inability to change the world. First of all, we can't do it because we ourselves are part of the problem. (Cue the eighties pop song "Man in the Mirror.") Paul makes this pointed observation about human nature in his letter to the Romans. In the tour de force tongue-twister of chapter 7, he laments, "For I do not do the good I want, but the evil I do not want is what I keep on doing. . . . So I find it to be a law that when I want to do right, evil lies close at hand. For I delight in the law of God, in my inner being, but I see in my members another law waging war against the law of my mind and making me captive to the law of sin that dwells in my members" (Rom 7:19-23). Wretched people that we are!

This is what Dave Zahl calls "low anthropology," a sober assessment of what it means to be human—our capacities, potentialities, and pitfalls. He contrasts this with a "high anthropology":

> A high anthropology views people as defined by their best days and greatest achievements, their dreams and their aspirations. A low anthropology assumes a through line of heartache and self-doubt, that the bulk of our mental energy is focused on subjects that would be embarrassing or even shameful if broadcast, and that our ability to do the right thing in any given situation is hampered by all sorts of unseen factors.[3]

The bottom line for this low anthropology is that we human creatures are simply much more limited than we'd like to imagine—and what's worse, the larger the scale of problems that we wish to fix, the greater the issues that we create. As Crouch quips, "Beware of world changers—they have not yet learned the true meaning of sin."[4]

This low anthropology points us toward another reason why we can't change the world, less nefarious than the first but no less consequential: we can't anticipate what's to come. The Epistle of James has the classic retort to inflated intentions about the future: "Come now, you who say, 'Today or tomorrow we will go into such and such a town and spend a year there and trade and make a profit'—yet you do not know what tomorrow will bring. What is your life? For you are a mist that appears for a little time and then vanishes" (Jas 4:13-14). Don't bother boasting about the fog.

I was reminded of this in a recent conversation with a colleague. We were getting into a deep talk about the future of the church and its institutions, what direction this or that societal trend was going, how we thought things would play out, and so on. There's something satisfying about those kinds of conversations; perhaps they provide some illusion of control. Which is why I appreciated—if also felt convicted—when at one point he paused, sighed, and said, "You know, I'm trying to learn to predict less and pray more." His admission reminded me of Yogi Berra's famous observation: "It is difficult to make predictions, especially about the future."

And this hints at one last reason why we can't change the world, perhaps most significant of all: *it's not our business*. As we discussed in chapter five, we sinful, silly humans are so prone to co-opting God's proper work for ourselves. Such foolishness is the product of pride, but it results in anxiety, frustration, and quiet desperation.

Once more, Andy Crouch writes, "Is there a way to change the world without falling into one of the many traps laid for would-be world changers? If so, it will require us to learn the one thing the language of 'changing the world' usually lacks: humility, defined not so much as bashfulness about our own abilities but as awed and quiet confidence in God's ability."[5]

Awed and quiet confidence in God's ability. God is God, I am not—and that's a good thing. He has not called you and me to change the world. That's his business; forget this, and we find ourselves back in the grip of the blasphemous anxiety, now writ large at a global scale. But if not that, then what *has* he called us to do?

Walking Gracefully

In this final part of the unambitious ambition, Paul identifies its goal, putting forth in the process an alternative to the restless, futile quest to change the world. Our aim instead, he says, is to "*walk gracefully* toward outsiders." We'll look more closely at the latter half of that phrase in chapter ten. Here, I want to ponder those first two words: walk gracefully.

Walking is the preferred metaphor in the Bible for the life of faith. Enoch famously "walked with God" (Gen 5:24). God enjoins the ninety-nine-year-old Abraham, "I am God Almighty; *walk* before me, and be blameless" (Gen 17:1). The Psalms often speak of it; for instance, "Teach me your way, O Lord, that I may *walk* in your truth; unite my heart to fear your name" (Ps 86:11). In Romans, Paul says that we were buried with Christ in baptism "in order that . . . we too might *walk* in newness of life" (Rom 6:4). And 2 Corinthians puts it straightforwardly: "We *walk* by faith, not by sight" (2 Cor 5:7). The path through Scripture is a pedestrian crossing.

The Bible also speaks at times of "running the race" (1 Cor 9:24; Heb 12:1, etc.) and, conversely, resting in God (Ex 31:15; Ps 127, etc.). Nevertheless, the overriding image to describe what it means to trust in Yahweh day to day is *walking*. "Walking is a beautiful metaphor used throughout Scripture to symbolize both movement and intimacy," writes Josh White for *Christianity Today*. "It is a lovely reminder that the goal of the Christian life is not arriving at a destination but knowing God. This is the very heart of what it means to be a disciple."[6]

And why should this be? Think about the nature of walking. On the one hand, it's a means of locomotion; you are moving forward, getting ahead. And yet, on the other hand, you are in no rush or hurry. It's simply one step at a time, one foot in front of the other—"power walking" has always struck me as a contradiction in terms. Walking is the natural pace and posture of the quiet ambition.

Like sharks and their necessary swimming, walking is the default way of being for God's human creatures. In walking, we go forward without getting ahead of the Lord Jesus, who carried out the entirety of his ministry, as others have pointed out, at three miles an hour.[7] By faith we thus travel at *Godspeed.* As Pastor Matt Canlis puts it in his moving documentary by that title, "We have to slow down to catch up with God."[8]

Walking therefore goes hand in hand with leading quiet lives of hope. What of this second word, *gracefully*? Admittedly, this isn't the typical translation of the phrase. More often you will see "walk properly" or (worse yet) "walk decently." Apart from being uninspiring English (when is the last time you noticed someone who had a decent walk?), this fails to capture the substance of the lovely Greek word that Paul employs.

Euschemonos has as its root word *schema*, "figure, shape, form" (cf. 1 Cor 7:31; Phil 2:8). The familiar prefix *eu-* means "good" or "well." When used as an adjective, then, the word has a meaning along the lines of "elegant figure, shapely, graceful." It's a word you'd use to describe a ballerina floating across the stage or an eagle flying over a lake. As an adverb, as it's being used in 1 Thessalonians 4:12, a fitting translation would be "becomingly" (ASV) or (less awkward and more resonant) "gracefully."

I especially like that latter translation for the way in which it captures the dual senses of the term. *Gracefully* means not only elegantly but also in a way marked by grace. This goes beyond the usage of the Greek term but is wholly appropriate theologically and in keeping with the point that Paul is making. The witness of Christians consists not in Herculean feats of world changing but in the humble feet of grace-filled steps.

Now, if you're anything like me, I know what you're thinking. All too often in my "Christian walk," I look less like a ballerina and more like a toddler (with all due respect to toddlers who may be reading). I fumble and I stumble and I fall on my face. Occasional flashes of inspiring Christian virtue aside, it often ain't all that pretty.

But here's where I'd lean on that latter connotation of "gracefully." What makes Christian witness appealing is not its moral rectitude; rather, it's when Christians live grace-filled, forgiveness-saturated lives. To be certain, virtue is admired and hypocrisy scorned. But lest we forget, the most grievous hypocrisy that Jesus decried was that of the Pharisees who tried to box out would-be believers from the kingdom; in other words, the hypocrisy was not a failure of *morals* but a failure of *mercy*.

All this to say, don't be scared off by the admonition to "walk gracefully." It's simpler and more salutary than you might think. Because when Christians strive to follow in the footsteps of their Savior, they walk gracefully toward outsiders and give a compelling Christian witness.

In other words, we can sow the seed and be the bean.

Coffee Bean Christians

In his book *The Coffee Bean*, author Jon Gordon recounts the modern fable of Abe, a young man who is stressed and filled with fear as he faces challenges in school and at home. There's a big test coming up and he's got Friday night's football game and his parents are constantly fighting, and it's a lot.

Abe's teacher, Mr. Jackson, sees the stress in his pupil's life. So one day after class Mr. Jackson has him stick around, and he asks Abe a strange question: "What happens when you put a carrot in really hot water?" Abe's befuddled. *Um, it gets hot?* The teacher tells Abe, go home and run the experiment for yourself. Abe reports back the next day: the carrot got soft.

Mr. Jackson, continuing his sage ways, asks, "Okay, now what if you put an *egg* in the boiling water?" Abe knows the answer to that without an experiment: you get a hard-boiled egg. That's right, Mr. Jackson affirms, the egg becomes hardened by its environment and the conditions it's in. By now Abe is starting to get hip to this lesson. But Mr. Jackson says, "I've got one more step for you. What happens when you put a coffee bean in really hot water?" Uncertain of the outcome, Abe takes some beans from Mr. Jackson and plans one more experiment.

The next day, Abe is eager to find Mr. Jackson after school and report his findings. The beans eventually turned the water into java—as with grounds in a Mr. Coffee, it just took a while longer. "It's like magic," Abe says. "It is," Mr. Jackson replies, "but I prefer to call it *transformation*." And then he continues:

> I want you to remember this lesson for the rest of your life. Wherever you go and whatever you do, remember you are a coffee bean and you have the power to transform any environment you are in. No matter how hard things get, or how hopeless things look, don't give up. Realize that we don't create our world from the outside in. We create and transform it from the inside out.[9]

It's a pleasant little fable, and even here the author is hard pressed not to lapse into the language of world changing. But the message is well taken and comports nicely with the unambitious ambition. After all, what does a coffee bean *do*? Is it anxiously trying to change the world, or even "transform its environment"? No, of course not. Its "witness," if you will, flows from its identity. What matters more than its activity is its simple, faithful *presence*.

Mustard Seed Conspiracy

"Faithful presence" is a phrase introduced into the Christian lexicon by sociologist James Davison Hunter in his seminal book *To Change the World*.[10] He introduces it as an alternative approach to the world-changing aspirations of either the Christian right (who focus on power), the Christian left (who focus on justice), or what he calls the Neo-Anabaptist (who focus on separation). Author Greg Thompson describes these respectively as the domination, accommodation, and fortification paradigms.[11]

Faithful presence, by contrast, reflects the love of the incarnate Lord, who "became flesh and dwelt among us" (Jn 1:14). "For the Christian," Hunter writes, "if there is a possibility for human flourishing in a world such as ours, it begins when God's word of love becomes flesh in us, is embodied in us, is enacted through us and in doing so, a trust is forged between the word spoken and the reality to which it speaks; to the words we speak and the realities to which we, the church, point."[12]

But we're spilling many words to say what Jesus said in precious few. "The kingdom of heaven is like a grain of mustard seed that a man took and sowed in his field," he says. "It is the smallest of all seeds, but when it has grown it is larger than all the garden plants and becomes a tree, so that the birds of the air come and make nests in its branches" (Mt 13:31-32). Faithful presence doesn't only mean being the bean but also being the seed—the *mustard* seed.

Walking gracefully, then, is like the mustard seed in motion. And as with the coffee bean, while actions are inextricably bound up with identity, the witness is principally a matter of faithful presence. To state the obvious: Jesus doesn't say you *should* be the light of the world, or you had *better be* the salt of the earth: he says *this is who you are*. By virtue of being joined to him in baptism, filled with the radiance of the Holy Spirit, you shine. You grow. You season.

That's why the collective mission of the people of God leading quiet lives of hope is a kind of mustard seed conspiracy.[13] It's Christians deployed into their many and various neighborhoods—whether that be on your block, in your school, at your workplace, or elsewhere—to shine light and show grace. We don't have to give people the full-on "Jesus-firehose," as pastor and author Greg Finke puts it; we just offer cups of cool water (Mt 10:42).[14]

To call this "coffee bean movement" of "mustard seed missionaries" a *conspiracy* suggests something subversive about it as well—and that's apt. Inasmuch as we are simultaneously pushing back on the destructive forces of the world and the discouraging work of the devil, there's a countercultural element to our walking gracefully.

In her book *Building the Benedict Option*, author Leah Libresco offers a humorous yet poignant analogy with the World War II–era *Simple Sabotage Field Manual*. The manual was created by the Office of Strategic Services (OSS) in order to aid allies in danger of Nazi occupation. Libresco notes how the handbooks don't advise readers to use explosives or effect other big, boisterous actions; rather they should do little things like leave tools out of place, clog up machines, or (my personal favorite) hinder decisions by handing them over to committees (!).

Libresco ties it together:

> The OSS's pupil is meant to seize every feasible opportunity, trusting that a thousand small acts of resistance will add up, instead of sitting on his hands, waiting for one big chance to act. Christians, too, should be panting (like the deer for running streams of Psalm 42) to offer any small act for the glory of God. Holding the door for an arthritic stranger, quietly praying for each person in your line of sight on a train or a bus, e-mailing a photo of a sacred artwork to a friend—each of these small things, done for God, becomes one strand in a tapestry of praise.[15]

Through the ages, God has upended the kingdoms of this world through the quiet lives of coffee bean Christians and mustard seed missionaries who walk gracefully and abide in faithful presence. What does that look like in practice? Let me offer a few brief examples from the Scriptures, church history, and my own parish experience.

The Mustard Seed Growing

The story of the mustard seed conspiracy starts in the book of Acts. There are plenty of remarkable miracles that accompanied the proclamation of Peter, Paul, and company. But what especially grabs the attention of outsiders is the simple life together of Christians under the canopy of God's grace: "Day by day, attending the temple together and breaking bread in their homes, they received their food with glad and generous hearts, praising God and having favor with all the people. And the Lord added to their number those who were being saved" (Acts 2:46-47).

This is not the kind of evangelism program one sometimes hears on offer nowadays. We are urged to take radical and inspiring measures to storm Hades's gates (and if those measures also happen to look good on social media, so much the better). But when Christians walk gracefully, with lightness in their steps and mercy in their manner, God does the heavy lifting of gathering souls into his kingdom.

The story of Acts continues into the growth of the church in the few centuries after Pentecost. Author Mike Aquilina points out the pivotal role played by Christian families, simply going about their everyday life. "In the beginning," he writes, "charity was . . . the way of Christian family life. This routine of charity did not so much constitute a new culture, replacing the old, at least externally. Outwardly, little had changed in the neighborhoods inhabited by Christians. The law, the government, the routines of daily life remained as they were—and as they would largely remain, intact, even after Constantine. But inwardly, everything had changed."

Drawing on a well-known early epistle, Aquilina points especially to the role played by Christian homes and families. He writes,

> The writer [of the Epistle to Diognetus] points out that Christians are not distinguished from other people by anything external: not their country or language, not their food or clothing, but by what he calls the Christians' "wonderful and striking way of life": "They marry, as do all others; they beget children; but they do not commit infanticide. They have a common table, but not a common bed. . . . They obey the prescribed laws, and at the same time surpass the laws by their lives. They love all men, and are persecuted by all. They are unknown and condemned; they are put to death, and restored to life. . . . To sum it up: as the soul is in the body, so Christians are in the world. . . . The invisible soul is guarded by the visible body, and Christians are known indeed to be in the world, but their godliness remains invisible."

Aquilina concludes: "That is what really happened to the Roman Empire. The gospel of Jesus Christ gradually spread, from person to person, from family to family, from home to home, from neighborhood to neighborhood, then to entire provinces. Conversion took place in the smallest increments, one by one."[16] As Saint Augustine put it: "The spread of the gospel is one heart setting another heart on fire."

I will give one more example from church history, this one much more modern. After the Bolshevik revolution in Russia, the Soviets attempted to stamp out Christian faith like they were extinguishing a campfire. In many respects they succeeded. Priests and bishops were routinely executed. Church buildings were repurposed for government functions or else demolished. And yet the flame of faith continued to flicker in the hearts of ordinary

Christians who kept walking gracefully—particularly in that subversive sort of way that Leah Libresco named.

A moving picture of what this looked like for some believers is painted by Amor Towles in his bestselling historical novel *A Gentleman in Moscow*. The narrator describes how a decommissioned church had a small chapel, which held a mosaic of Christ and the woman at the well (Jn 4) that no one had bothered to dismantle. Day by day an interminable line for food rations snaked through the sanctuary. Meanwhile, Towles writes, "The women who waited in line for their milk were willing to hold your place while you slipped away to pray."[17] Like the Hebrew midwives, the Russian women managed to submit to their masters and still keep faith.

Sociologist Peter Berger recounts an even bolder profession. From time to time, he writes, the Communist Party conducted campaigns to propagate "scientific atheism." The Christians of the village would have to assemble in front of the church and submit to a ritual harangue about the supposed illusions of religion. But Berger tells of one such instance in which the Soviets got more than they bargained for:

> The commissar made a generous gesture and said that the priest had five minutes for a rebuttal. The priest came forward and said, "I don't need five minutes." He then turned to the assembled villagers and said, "Christ is risen!" They replied with the proper liturgical formula: "He is risen indeed!" The priest then returned to his place in the congregation.[18]

Over and again in the history of the church, the world has been changed by God alone moving mountains through the humble yet heroic efforts of human beings. He does it not by means of large levers but by little acts. By the faithful presence of coffee bean Christians, walking gracefully (if boldly) toward outsiders. And sometimes, as I have witnessed in my ministry, by taking the notion of the coffee bean even more literally.

The Neighborly Café

Kurt and Tammy were a newly retired couple in one of the congregations that I served. They had noticed that our small town could really use a coffee shop—the fabled "third place," where neighbors could get together for a cuppa and conversation. In the wintertime especially, when snowbirds take flight and the town feels like it empties out, loneliness and isolation can easily set in. Wouldn't it be great, Kurt and Tammy thought, if there were a place where folks could still gather during the week.

The problem was that, as one steely-eyed businessman told us, there simply weren't enough rooftops in town to support a viable year-round coffee shop: you'd never make any money. But Kurt and Tammy were undeterred. They thought, why does it have to be a full-fledged coffee shop? People just want to sit together and talk. That hardly takes any staff or fancy machinery.

And so, inspired by our Sunday coffee hour at church, they launched the Neighborly Café, a twice-a-week coffee klatch held in the parish hall (or, during the summer, out on the church's front lawn), with middling church coffee and delectable baked goods donated by church ladies. And a heavy dose of laughter, gossip, and conversation.

The Neighborly Café never set the world on fire. On any given day, a dozen or so folks came through, including a number of regulars. I think once there was close to thirty and we ran out of cookies. But I recall one regular in particular, Debra. Debra was a new widow in her eighties. She lived off of a meager Social Security check and heated her home through the winter from wood that her son cut from the back forty. When the flakes flew she'd just as soon hole up in her house and wait it out till May, most years. But that first winter after her husband died, she knew something had to change.

That's when Kurt started inviting her to come out to the Neighborly Café. She begged off at first, but then turned up on a December morning . . . and every morning hence that the coffee was on and the cookies set out. Debra became not just a regular but a staple. She often didn't say much; she'd sit and listen to the stories and unvarnished opinions from some of the old duffers. Occasionally she'd correct this or that detail of local lore. But mostly she'd just sit and sip her coffee with a Mona Lisa smile.

When that first winter without her late husband finally came to an end, I heard a knock at the door of my study. "You know, I'd probably be dead without this little coffee club," Debra said. "I told Kurt already, but I just wanted to say thank you. It saved my life." Even more than the Folgers in my cup, that was the best part of waking up that day.

We strive to walk gracefully, because there's a lot of quiet desperation out there. Folks like Debra, who feel hope seeping out like warmth from an old house. The world needs coffee bean Christians like Kurt and Tammy, who'll keep the pot hot and the conversation percolating. With a drip, drip, drip, the well of hope begins to refill.

10

THEM THAT ARE WITHOUT

Wise is the country parson that always seeks to make nice with his neighbors. After all, when you are not only a pastor but you live in the parsonage right next door to church, it's as if your whole existence were one of those Jesus-fish appliques that Christians used to put on their bumpers, advertising your identity. (What happened to those, anyway?) It can be an occupational hazard.

For the most part, though, in my years of parish ministry my family has handled it well. The kids have been reasonably respectful, the dog has only gotten loose to chase passersby a couple of times, and I, of course, have *always* been a paragon of virtue on my very best behavior. We have been, by all accounts, model Christian neighbors. Or so I thought.

And then we got chickens. We were living at the time in a rural village, if not the country per se, and so chickens seemed a natural addition. We'd had them at a previous parish that was decidedly more urban; surely building a coop and keeping a handful of hens would be no problem, right? In our quiet town, we could even let them free range through the neighborhood. Alas, that was our mistake.

One day I started getting a flurry of text messages from a neighbor who lived a stone's throw away from church. He and his wife had been upset a couple of years prior about our church bells, which rang on the hour during the day and chimed a few hymns at noon and six. We did our best to work through that kerfuffle in a spirit of Christian charity and neighborliness, but suffice it to say that this couple had no love lost toward the church or its parsonage-inhabiting pastor.

So I start receiving this slew of texts from the neighbor complaining that the chickens were tearing up his yard and pooping in his garden. (I wanted to tell him that people pay good money for chicken poop to put in their garden, but I demurred.) I was away from home making a visit at the time, but I shot a message to Anne to ask if she could handle it.

My wife, Anne, is a remarkable woman in so many ways. But not even Proverbs 31 mentions the wife who is able to wrangle a half-dozen chickens who are trolling the neighborhood and restore them to their coop. It's a feat of intrepid bravery and agility. But she did it. And what's more, she collected a dozen fresh eggs, crated them, and wrote a heartfelt note of apology to take over to the upset neighbors.

She approached the back door, and before she could even knock, the wife opened it. Standing in the shadows of her hallway, still behind the closed screen door and before a word was on Anne's tongue, the woman said that she didn't want any of our eggs—and shut the door in Anne's face. My dear sweet wife put the eggs and the note on the stoop and left, nearly in tears. And no, I didn't return in the night with my boys to throw the eggs at the house. Because we're Christians. But I won't say it didn't cross my mind.

You have interactions like that with the world and with your neighbors, and it's enough to make you throw up your hands and say, "To hell with them! (Literally.) I'm just going to live apart, focus on my own self, fashion my coffee table, and pursue my personal quiet life. As for the outsiders—they can fend for themselves."

You might call it the Jonah option.

The Jonah Option

There are few characters in the Bible more frustrating and more familiar than the prophet Jonah. Frustrating because he throws tantrums like a two-year-old, evading (or trying to evade) the call of God; familiar because, well, so do we (we're just more subtle about it). But his story has a larger resonance within biblical history on down to our own enactment of the quiet ambition today.

Jonah is given a great gift: membership among the elect people of God. Let's not forget that such status is ever and always conferred, received, and never achieved. But in any case, he possesses it. Straightaway, God calls on Jonah to put that privilege to use: go and bear witness to pagan Nineveh, he says. And famously, Jonah does nearly the exact opposite, boarding the first ship for Tarshish, far from the city of his calling. He'd prefer not to face the challenge.

Subsequently, we find Jonah asleep in the stern, satisfied with the success of his evasion. But God is not so easily avoided. A great storm compels a grudging witness from Jonah to the ship's crew—"I am a Hebrew, and I fear the Lord, the God of heaven, who made the sea and the dry land" (Jon 1:9)—who eventually throw him overboard and, wonder of wonders, are brought to faith in the process. Almost as though God were saying to Jonah, "My mission will be accomplished; would you rather we do it the easy way or the hard way?"

Jonah has chosen the hard way. Retreat is what he wanted, and now he has all the peace and quiet he can swallow inside the belly of a large fish. Contrite, he cries out to God, who takes counsel with the fish—which then spews him back onto dry land. When the summons to Nineveh is repeated, Jonah doesn't delay. And in a miraculous act of God, the middling prophet's proclamation manages to evoke repentance among all the people of that great city.

For all this, Jonah throws a pity party on the outskirts of town. It all happened just as he feared. The Lord once again favored the outsider and failed to let Jonah keep the blessing to himself. All he wanted was to mind his own business and let Nineveh get what it undoubtedly had coming to it. Alas, the Lord is merciful and gracious, slow to anger and abounding in steadfast love, and his purpose will win out.

Now, why do I bother to recount this famous story? First, because as the great missiologist Lesslie Newbigin points out, Jonah's story is the sad, sordid story of Israel in a nutshell. "The meaning of Israel's election and of its misunderstanding of it is depicted with supreme dramatic power in the story of Jonah, which is perhaps the most moving interpretation of the missionary calling of God's people to be found in the Bible."[1] Newbigin goes on to point out how, just as Jonah (emblematic of the people of God) is called to bear witness in Nineveh (emblematic of the pagan world opposed to God), so also Israel as a whole had the privilege and calling to be "a kingdom of priests and a holy nation" (Ex 19:6).

Throughout the Scriptures we see the people of God succumbing to this temptation. *Hide it under a bushel? Sure, why not!* They become preoccupied with their own concerns, blind to the needs of their neighbors (if at the same time all too often enamored with their neighbors' gods). Thus the thundering of the prophets down through the ages. For instance, Isaiah:

> They seek me daily
>   and delight to know my ways,

as if they were a nation that did righteousness
    and did not forsake the judgment of their God;
they ask of me righteous judgments;
    they delight to draw near to God.
"Why have we fasted, and you see it not?
    Why have we humbled ourselves, and you take no
        knowledge of it?"
Behold, in the day of your fast you seek your own pleasure,
    and oppress all your workers. . . .
Is not this the fast that I choose:
    to loose the bonds of wickedness,
    to undo the straps of the yoke,
to let the oppressed go free,
    and to break every yoke?
Is it not to share your bread with the hungry
    and bring the homeless poor into your house;
when you see the naked, to cover him,
    and not to hide yourself from your own flesh?
Then shall your light break forth like the dawn,
    and your healing shall spring up speedily;
your righteousness shall go before you;
    the glory of the LORD shall be your rear guard.
        (Is 58:2-3, 6-8)

The story of Old Testament Israel is the story in large part of a people who fail to live with a view toward outsiders.

But I tell Jonah's story, secondly and more pointedly, because his story is also *our* story. Even though we all know from Sunday school that Jonah was in the wrong, gussied up versions of fleeing the scary and reprobate world persist. Indeed, this may be the chief temptation facing the people of God as we seek to lead quiet lives of hope: to turn our back on outsiders. To so focus on the lives that *we* want that we lose sight of those who are without.

It is certainly the case that, as many authors have pointed out in recent years, Christians in the West now find themselves in a world that bears some resemblance to that of the early Christians (and Old Testament prophets). We're surrounded by an increasingly pagan and even anti-Christian society; the "negative world," as author Aaron Renn has put it.[2] It's natural to want to retreat, and in some respects—as we saw especially with respect to the "noisemakers" of contemporary society—even necessary (think back to chapter three).

Even so, this last part of the quiet ambition counteracts the urge toward the more flagrant manifestations of the Jonah option. Paul simply won't let us walk away from the world when he says, "Make it your ambition to live quietly . . . so that you might walk gracefully *toward outsiders*."

Them That Are Without

It's hard for me to hear about "the outsiders" without thinking of middle school English class or the Brat Pack. With all due respect to Emilio Estevez, though, Paul's appeal is even more compelling.[3] His Greek can be literally translated "those who are on the outside." I appreciate the somewhat archaic language of the King James translation: "them that are without." It's a felicitous convergence of connotations, however, since oftentimes those who are on the outside are "them that are without." But we might ask: without *what?*

Jesus tells parables, he says, because outsiders "may indeed hear but not *understand*" (Mk 4:12, emphasis added). He feels compassion for the crowds "because they were harassed and helpless, like sheep without a *shepherd*" (Mt 9:36, emphasis added). Apart from him, outsiders are alienated from heavenly citizenship and foreigners to the promise, "having no *hope* and without *God* in the world" (Eph 2:12, emphasis added). Yet for all this, due to their sinful rebellion and spiritual pride, they are "without *excuse*" (Rom 1:20, emphasis added).

I have spoken of outsiders in the *third* person plural—them—but faith starts in the *first* person plural—us—or indeed the forceful singular: *I*. *I* was the outsider, *I* was the one without hope and without excuse. Yet to this end Christ came: to make the outsiders insiders, to give hope to them who are without. To save even *me*.

Foretelling his own destiny, Jesus relates the story of the wicked tenants (Mt 21:33-46; Mk 12:1-12; Lk 20:9-19). The faithful owner of the vineyard repeatedly sends servants to his tenants when it comes time to harvest fruit. Alas, they beat one, stone another, run each and all out of town with their tails between their legs. But then, this blessedly stubborn master resolves, "I will send my son." When he does, however, it's just another episode of Tenants Behaving Badly: they took the son and cast him *outside*—and killed him (Mt 21:39).

Jesus' fate awaited him "outside." Thus the author of Hebrews reminds us that just as the bodies of the animal sacrifices of old were burned outside the camp, "so Jesus also suffered outside the gate in order to sanctify the people through his own blood" (Heb 13:12). He who was "without *sin*"; the Lamb of God "without *blemish*" (Heb 4:15; 1 Pet 1:19, emphasis added). Jesus, the ultimate insider, the very son of God, blessed within the bosom of the Father, went without to bring the outsiders in.

This is why we who endeavor to lead quiet lives of hope walk gracefully toward "them that are without." Because that's where we meet Jesus. In the overlooked and the undervalued. In the "last, the little, the lost, and the least," to invoke Robert Farrar Capon's collection of the objects of God's affection.[4] Once more, from Hebrews: "Therefore let us go to him [Christ] outside the camp" (Heb 13:13).

Christians are those who pour themselves out for the sake of them that are without. We are like "living sacrifices," Scripture tells us. Think of the Old Testament sacrifices and picture a basin filled with blood. The priests were instructed that the blood of the sacrifices be "poured out" at the base of the altar (Ex 29:12; Lev 4:30; Deut 12:27, etc.). By faith we are like those holy vessels, pouring ourselves out. Filled with the Holy Spirit, though, we are continually replenished, continually renewed. There's always more to give when what we give is not our own.

Growing Responsibility

But as we near the conclusion of our consideration of the quiet ambition, a fresh tension here arises that brings us full circle. For if you maintain concern for them that are without—and you should!—then you make yourself susceptible to being called on in new and even seemingly *ambitious* ways: not for your own benefit but for the benefit of others. The needs of a dying world are vast and consequential; the Master may thus have need for you in ways you don't anticipate.

Think of the story Jesus tells that may speak most directly to the topic of ambition, the so-called parable of the wedding feast (Lk 14:7-11). The context is that the Lord had been invited to dine at the house of a ruler of the Pharisees. Even more than a black-tie gala in our day and age, a meal such as this in Jesus' time was an occasion to jockey for position. Demonstrate your status. Who has the highest seat? Who's the guy in charge? And who's low man on the ladder?

But Jesus turns this on its head. He says that when you're invited to a wedding feast, don't sit in the place of honor. Rather, "go and sit in the lowest place," he advises (Lk 14:10). Practice humility. Live quietly. Don't elbow for position but rather exalt others. Prideful as we are, we all need to hear and heed this word repeatedly. The summons to lower yourself to lift up others can't be stressed enough.

And yet Jesus doesn't end the teaching there. He goes on to say, "When your host comes he may say to you, 'Friend, move up higher.' Then you will be honored in the presence of all who sit at table with you" (Lk 14:10). Honored, yes, and also entrusted with greater stewardship. For the high seat doesn't merely mean prestige. It means responsibility. It means caring for the others at the table.

This is also the message of the parable of the talents, which we looked at in chapter one. For those servants that take the trust given them by the master and multiply their talents, they're not only given commendation; they're given a new commission. "Well done, good and faithful servant," the master says. "You have been faithful over a little; I will set you over much" (Mt 25:23). In the economy of the kingdom, the reward for faithfulness is not retirement but responsibility.

This pattern can be observed again and again—in the Bible, in Christian history, in everyday life. Those who seek to faithfully occupy the lowest seat get called up to a higher one. This is not a strategy for getting ahead; it's a statement of the way things work according to God's providence. To be sure, there are plenty of selfishly ambitious people who scratch and scrape to climb every rung of the ladder and end up in "the highest seat." But it is precisely those who *don't* feel the need to call the shots, to be in charge, to claim acclaim, whom the world needs to lead.

So what might this mean in your life? It may look like accepting a promotion at work in which you'll have the platform to promote the flourishing of the organization and your peers. Or it may look like the opportunity to take on a position of leadership at your church, which you neither sought nor even perhaps desired, but in which your particular expertise is needed for the congregation's well-being. Or it may even look like something as simple folks wishing to tap you as the first president of the new neighborhood association. Go figure.

In these and innumerable other ways, great and small, followers of Jesus who lead quiet lives of hope for the sake of them that are without may well be asked to "come up higher" and take on increasing responsibility. It's part of the paradox of the unambitious ambition. When you live quietly and walk gracefully, you may well be called on to serve in new ways and, indeed, be given fresh opportunities. Should you refuse? Is it a betrayal of the quiet ambition if you accept? And how do you discern what is a call from God in your life and what is your own personal aspiration?

These are big questions in their own right, and to explore them fully would take another book. For now, let me offer a case study from a lesser-known moment of a larger-than-life disciple of Jesus, Dietrich Bonhoeffer.

Dietrich's Dilemma

Dietrich Bonhoeffer had little sympathy for the Jonah option. In a potent passage from his classic work *Discipleship*, Bonhoeffer reflects on Martin Luther's exodus from monasticism and into public life, after the Reformer rediscovered the richness of the gospel message:

> Luther's path out of the monastery back to the world meant the sharpest attack that had been launched on the world since early Christianity. The rejection which the monk had given the world was child's play compared to the rejection that the world endured through his returning to it. This time the attack was a frontal assault. Following Jesus now had to be lived out in the midst of the world.[5]

In a moment from his life that is not as well-known as the drama that would later envelop him, Bonhoeffer himself faced a fork in the road not altogether unlike the one that Luther did when departing the monastery. In 1933, Bonhoeffer left his native Germany amid the strife that was engulfing the nation and the church. For the first time in his career, he assumed the full-time post of a parish pastor, ministering to two small Lutheran congregations (St. George's and St. Paul's) in a suburb southeast of London.

Life was peaceful for Bonhoeffer in England. No longer directly under the authority of the Reich church, he experienced a freedom to speak and preach that had been denied him. This is not to say that Bonhoeffer was kicking his feet up; to the contrary, he worked vigorously on behalf of Christians back in Germany, returning to the continent at least once a month.[6] What's more, Bonhoeffer was diligent in his duties to the parish: he would pour himself out in preaching and teaching, start a Sunday school and youth group, and "single-handedly revive the languishing St. George's choir."[7]

Even so, he was outside the bubbling cauldron of Germany, and life was pleasant for him. He enjoyed the simplicity of parish life and the peaceful beauty of the English country. More acutely, he wasn't in danger! He could tend to his own business and live more or less as he pleased. He wasn't exactly in Tarshish, but he certainly had avoided Nineveh for a season.

And yet the events back home and the plight of those who were outside his peaceful bubble gnawed at him. He wrote to a friend, "I am hopelessly torn between staying here . . . and returning to Germany to take charge of a preachers' seminary shortly to be opened there."[8] He had been asked to return to his homeland and start a new school for pastors of the Confessing Church.

Around this time, Bonhoeffer's friend and mentor, Karl Barth, wrote to him a pointed and compelling letter:

> I have no intention of regarding your going off to England as anything other than a perhaps personally necessary interlude . . . What is all this about "going into the wilderness," and "the quietness of pastoral work," etc., at a moment when you are wanted in Germany? . . . Under no circumstances should you now be playing Elijah under the juniper tree or Jonah under the gourd; you need to be here with all guns blazing! . . .
>
> This is just not the time to grow weary. So is it even less the time to go to England! What in all the world are you supposed to be doing or hoping to do there? Just be glad I don't have you here in front of me, because then I'd find an entirely different way of putting it to you forcefully that you need to drop all these quirks and special considerations, however fascinating, and think only of one thing: that you are a German, that your church's house is on fire, that you know enough, and know well enough how to say what you know, to be able to help, and in fact you ought to return to your post by the next ship![9]

Bonhoeffer would prove to be more Jeremiah than Jonah. It was the former who professed, "If I say, 'I will not mention him, or speak any more in his name,' there is in my heart as it were a burning fire shut up in my bones, and I am weary with holding it in, and I cannot" (Jer 20:9). In a sermon on that "weeping prophet" while he was yet in England, Bonhoeffer said, "Jeremiah was not eager to become a prophet of God. When the call came to him all of a sudden, he shrank back, he resisted, he tried to get away. . . . Not to be able to get away from God is the constant *disquieting* thing in the life of every Christian."[10]

Bonhoeffer felt the burning in his bones and the burden of God's call laid on his own life, and he returned to Germany to fulfill his task. It would ultimately result in his imprisonment and execution by the Nazis as he sought to be faithful to Christ's summons to discipleship.[11]

Lessons from Bonhoeffer

Bonhoeffer's experience was extraordinary and its circumstances dramatic. Lord willing, none of us will ever have to face such a crucible. But while the stakes were unique to him, the shape of his decision is instructive for us all. There are lessons for any of us who seek to walk gracefully toward outsiders and be faithful to God's claim on our lives.

First of all, Bonhoeffer was supremely sensitive to the plight of them that were without. He didn't stop his ears to the cries of his countrymen who were struggling, including his own family. So also for us, the starting point is the needs of our neighbors and the requirements of God's kingdom. We take sober assessment of the place where we are and the people among whom we live and ask, What is their plight? How are they in pain? And how am I being called on to serve here?

Second, then, Bonhoeffer was honest about his own equipping. God had given Bonhoeffer gifts, talents, and experiences that made him uniquely suited for the mission at hand. So also we ought to "listen to our lives," as Frederick Buechner put it, to hear in them the frequency of the Almighty as transmitted through our particular experience. To quote Buechner's famous maxim: "The place God calls you to is the place where your deep gladness and the world's deep hunger meet."[12]

Third, Bonhoeffer listened not only to his life but also to wise counselors. Karl Barth was a trusted mentor who had a more objective vantage point from which to speak into Bonhoeffer's life—and he took heed. As we ponder how best to put our own skills to use in service to the kingdom, we do well to give an ear to friends, pastors, teachers: people who have poured into our lives and possess a perspective on the larger sweep of the Lord's work in it.

Fourth and finally, Bonhoeffer recognized that his call was to discipleship and to following Christ Jesus, come what may. What particularly strikes me about this is that the common trope of our culture is to focus on what I want, as if I were the author of my own story.[13] Bonhoeffer's example reminds us that our prayer is *Thy* will be done. What matters most is what *God* wants, not me. As Saint Paul put it, "Therefore we also have as our ambition, whether at home or absent, to be pleasing to Him" (2 Cor 5:9 NASB).

To desire and aspire to live quiet and peaceful lives is a good and godly thing. It is too rarely sought and appreciated in our restless, noisy age. Even so, Bonhoeffer's story reminds us that it is not an ultimate thing. Only the kingdom of God is ultimate. We followers of Jesus are all of us servants of the King who serve at his pleasure. He may well summon you to serve in a new way, in a new place, among new people. So long as you are a soldier in the Lord's army, you are ever and always a member of his standing reserves, subject to his call.

The quiet ambition is not dependent on circumstances. It's a posture of spirit more than it is a place of residence. Wherever we are and in whatever station of life, we aspire to live quietly and walk gracefully toward them that are without. That may mean something as gravely consequential as that you are called to help lead your church through perilous times. Or, to return to where we began this chapter, it may mean something as simple as delivering some eggs to your neighbor.

The Rest of the Story

Congregations that I've served have always been filled with saints who sought to be good neighbors and share God's heart for the neighborhood. One of the ways this was done in the aforementioned parish with our free-range chickens was to plant a small community garden in the church's backyard. We started it with some trepidation, though, because of our disgruntled neighbors, and we didn't want to provoke any more dust-ups. But Ruth, the gal who was spearheading the garden ministry, reached out to make sure all was well and she received a green light.

Over that summer, the wife of the neighboring couple would peek her head out the door from time to time to see the progress. Walking down the alleyway, she might stop to comment on how nice the tomatoes looked. Once, when someone accidentally left on the sprinkler, she took it upon herself to turn it off so that the budding veggies weren't drowned.

And then one day, while Ruth was out doing some weeding, the woman came by with a request. She walked up gingerly, like she was interrupting a board meeting, and asked if she could help out in the garden. Ruth flashed a broad smile and in her welcoming, grandmotherly way said, "Yes, of course! We'd love to have you!"

The neighbor let out a sigh of relief. She shared that it had been a hard year for her, and that she was so taken aback by Anne's graceful response to her unkindness that it moved her to want to pitch in if she could. Who would have thought?

Neighbors can be a pain, but they're also people who are in pain. That's why, when we lead quiet lives of hope, we do so with a view toward outsiders who are themselves often mired in quiet desperation. In that place of deep hunger, God calls us to bring to bear our deep gladness in him for the blessing of them that are without.

The Practice of Walking Gracefully

The unambitious ambition is not a charge to change the world, nor to avoid it, but rather a calling to give quiet, winsome witness by walking gracefully toward outsiders. We are part of the mustard seed conspiracy; we are watching and waiting for the work of our King—and even if he might call us forth to serve in fresh ways.

Suggestions for practicing the quiet ambition

1. **Sow seeds.** One way to be reminded of the slow work of God is to behold it in creation. Plant some seeds, whether of mustard or magnolias, and watch them grow . . . slowly. It takes the time it takes. Gardening is also a great outlet for working with your hands, for many of the same reasons that baking bread is, with the added benefit that it's (generally) outdoors.
2. **Listen to your life.** When we get in the groove of everyday life, it's easy to stop asking the big questions about one's calling and daily work. Take some time to tune into the Lord's frequency and "listen to your life," as Frederick Buechner advises.

    - Read the parables of the wedding feast (Lk 14:7-11) and the talents (Mt 25:14-30), and pray back to the Lord how he speaks to you in them.

- Reflect on Dietrich Bonhoeffer's story. What elements of it resonate with your own experience? How does it inspire or challenge you? Jot down some of your thoughts.
- Invite a trusted friend or mentor out for coffee. Tell them you'd like for them to speak into your life and provide godly guidance: Do they see you using your gifts well, or might there be additional or alternative outlets for service? Talk about what it might mean for you to "be the bean" as you enjoy some java.

3. **Take a Sunday afternoon saunter.** That noted pedestrian Henry David Thoreau observes in his essay "Walking" that *saunter* came from a French word describing pilgrims that were traveling *a la Sainte Terre*, to the Holy Land. Go on a Sunday afternoon saunter of your own. Talk to the Lord or with your spouse. Take your time. Make your way toward the new creation.
4. **Heap burning coals.** The apostle Paul (echoing Proverbs) encourages disciples, "If your enemy is hungry, feed him; if he is thirsty, give him something to drink; for by so doing you will heap burning coals on his head" (Rom 12:20). Practicing mercy provides a compelling witness to your neighbors.
   - My wife has shown me, and not only once, the wisdom of Paul's injunction to extend kindness in the face of opposition. Who inspires you in your witness? Write out a list of people who make you want to be a more faithful, grace-filled disciple of Jesus. Consider reaching out and letting them know they have had this effect.
   - Lay to heart those people who are problematic in your life—at work, in the neighborhood, perhaps even in your own family. In keeping with Jesus' directive, make it a

point this week to "pray for those who persecute you" (Mt 5:44).

- And do good to those who are difficult. You probably have your own disgruntled neighbors in your life. Take her some eggs; bring him a token of kindness. Foil the devil by showing mercy.

Conclusion

THINK LITTLE

IN A LITTLE OUT-OF-THE-WAY PLACE on the Old Mission Peninsula of northern Michigan there's a secret garden. My wife and I visited for a recent wedding anniversary. The garden teems with poppies and azaleas and roses and lavender. Especially lavender.

The garden has a shop filled with all manner of lavender gifts: soaps and balms and ice cream and much more. One sort of gift especially caught my eye since it seemed so out of place. On a shelf tucked in the corner were some darling figurines, handcrafted by local Benedictine nuns. Carved from balsa wood and individually painted, the figurines depicted heroes of the faith from Scripture and church history such as Mary, Joseph, Mother Teresa, and more. Each came with a small pouch of lavender, complete with a tiny cross inside, which you could put in your pocket as a prompt to pray.

My wife noticed me admiring the figurines and bought the one of Saint Thérèse of Lisieux, the "Little Flower." (Saints and boxers get cool nicknames.) As it turns out, she couldn't have chosen more perfectly.

Thérèse became a Carmelite nun in Lisieux, France, at the precocious age of fifteen. From her earliest days, she sensed a call on her life to seek God fully. As she would later write, "I don't want to be a saint by halves. . . . My God, I choose all." At the tender age of twenty-three she was stricken with tuberculosis, however, and at twenty-four she was dead. Her bright light burned out far too soon.

Such a story would seem to be the quintessential stuff of quiet disappointment with God. A life of so much promise and potential—snuffed out before she had the chance to leave her mark. And yet this short-lived French nun was beatified quicker than Joan of Arc and dubbed by Pope Pius X "the greatest saint of modern times."[1] How could the Little Flower leave such a lasting impression?

Where there's a will, as the old saying goes, there's a way—in this case, a Little Way. This is the name Thérèse gave for what she called her "theory of love." The Little Way for her meant following Jesus in the midst of mundane annoyances and quotidian tasks. She called them "trial runs": ignoring the slight of a fellow nun who barred her from mother superior; showing kindness to a sister whose teeth-clicking vexed her to no end; demonstrating patience toward messy nuns (evidently they exist); and even relinquishing ownership of her own spiritual insights when she overhears other nuns claiming them as their own.[2]

In an essay reflecting on the significance of Saint Thérèse for believers today, Richard Lischer writes:

> Her Little Way is accessible, just as the little stories Jesus told are accessible to those with ears to hear. According to his parables, if you cannot practice love amidst the routine crises of village and family life, you will never attain to a higher spirituality, because there is none. It is the little ones, not the big, who will enter the kingdom of God. It is the Little Way or No Way. By narrating the smallest and least complicated moments in her own life, Thérèse opens a door onto everyday holiness and invites the least of us to enter.[3]

Though I'm a Protestant Christian, I'm tempted to call Saint Thérèse the patron saint of quiet ambition. It's no accident, after all, that she became the namesake of another Teresa, one better known in our day, who said, We can do no great things, only "small things with great love."[4] Her story is a fitting place to start as we conclude our exploration of living quietly in this noisy age.

The figurine of Saint Thérèse now rests on the desk of my study. Encircling its base is a quote from the Little Flower: "When one loves, one doesn't calculate." It's hard to imagine a more countercultural message.

Going Infinite

He seemed like such a nice young man. When journalist Michael Lewis first met the now disgraced bitcoin investor Sam Bankman-Fried, he was taken by the demeanor of the one colloquially known as SBF: "[Sam] hadn't been warped by money in the ways people often are. He wasn't braggy. He had opinions, but he didn't seem to expect his listener to share them, and he pretended to listen to mine even when what I was saying clearly didn't interest him." Everything about Bankman-Fried was unassuming, even to a fault; his disheveled look of cargo shorts, ratty T-shirts, and sprawling, unkempt hair would come back to bite him in the court of public opinion. But it was true to his personality. "His ambition was grandiose," writes Lewis, "but he wasn't."[5]

So what was that grandiose ambition? In short, to maximize the number of lives he could "save" (though not in any spiritual sense) by making as much money as possible and then applying those dollars to the world's problems. Already a billionaire when Lewis met him, SBF was asked the natural question reminiscent of the famous exchange with the twentieth-century baron John D. Rockefeller: How much will be enough? Unlike Rockefeller's ruefully honest claim—"one dollar more"—SBF was blunt: he had use for "infinity dollars."

Lewis writes, "He needed infinity dollars because he planned to address the biggest existential risks to life on earth: nuclear war, pandemics far more deadly than Covid, artificial intelligence that turned on mankind and wiped us out, and so on."[6] In contrast to your stereotypical billionaire, content with accruing houses, jewelry, and various vessels of transportation, SBF wanted much more: "It felt unambitious to not care about what happened to the rest of the world. . . . It was shooting too low to only think about what was going to impact me."[7]

SBF fell in with leading proponents of a movement that has come to be known as "effective altruism": *altruism* because it is putatively aimed at doing good for others; *effective* because it is focused on accomplishing change at a massive scale. While this all sounds well and good—and undoubtedly some good things have been done through it—effective altruism has some fatal flaws that are made manifest in the lives of its most notable exponents. (SBF was convicted of fraud and conspiracy in March 2024.)[8]

Psychiatrist George Lerner has become the world's leading authority on the inner life of effective altruists as a result of his connection to the leaders in cryptocurrency through his Bay Area practice. "They all professed to care about 'humanity,'" Lerner tells Lewis, "while at the same time often being a bit slow to love actual people."[9] What Lerner encountered among the effective altruism set was a band of individuals who looked at the world like a math problem, the solution to which was to go bigger; if possible, to go *infinite.*

Raising the Little

There is an undeniable allure to the vision of SBF and the effective altruists. It's the vision of grand scale and maximal impact, of calculating and manipulating. It's one more gambit for escaping quiet desperation: chasing meaningfulness through bigness and significance by size. Lord knows we Christians, especially pastors, can fall prey to this. Chad Bird writes, "Nothing says success in modern Christianity more than being the biggest church in town. . . . We have assumed, almost without question, that bigger is better. It's as if retail giants have become patron saints of the church, as if the superstore model is the super-church model."[10]

It is an alluring vision, I say, but by no means the only one. I have come to believe that a more excellent way is that which is embodied in quiet lives of hope that can be witnessed among ordinary saints in churches around the world. In its own way it follows the tradition of the Little Way. In an essay from nearly fifty years ago, which is only more resonant today, Wendell Berry wrote, "For most of the history of this country our motto, implied or spoken, has been Think Big. A better motto, and an essential one, is Think Little."[11]

Think little. Berry himself exemplifies the motto. While his work has reached a wide audience and made an immeasurable impact in the lives of his readers (yours truly included), Berry has tended to his business at home. He has been devoted to his family, cared for his farm and community, nurtured words as if they were dear friends. His grand vision for a society that is richer and more rooted, committed to neighborliness and the wisdom of the ancient paths, is undeniably ambitious; his application of it, unambitiously so.

So it is for any of us seeking to live quietly. Thinking little makes me think of the widow who donated two little coins into the offering box. Chump change, people might have thought. But Jesus, calling the disciples to himself, sets the record straight: "Truly, I say to you, this poor widow has put in more than all those who are contributing to the offering box. For they all contributed out of their abundance, but she out of her poverty has put in everything she had, all she had to live on" (Mk 12:43-44). Her gift wasn't so small, after all.

Or I think of one of Hollywood's most poignant depictions of quiet ambition, *It's a Wonderful Life*, and its hero George Bailey. George was "an intelligent, smart, ambitious young man"—the despicable despot Mr. Potter himself said as much. But as the chasm opened wider between George's expectations for how his life would look and his reality, he started to sink in the quicksand of quiet desperation. It took an angel named Clarence and a vision of what life might have been like had he never been born for George to realize that as he served his customers at the old Building and Loan, attended to his neighbors in Bedford Falls, honored his parents, and cared for his wife and family—that in that unambitious life he proved himself "the richest man in town."[12]

Or I think of Howard Hart. I heard his story on the delightful podcast *What It's Like to Be*, hosted by Dan Heath.[13] Howard spent three decades as a stadium beer vendor. Grunt work if ever there was, right? Some of his family members even told him that he squandered his life; he had so much untapped potential, they said. And yet Howard created community in the sections of the stadiums he served. He built relationships that have spanned decades. He learned the names of his regular customers, sent them Christmas cards, even helped one man overcome his alcoholism. Given his evident faith, I don't think it would be too much of a stretch to say Howard carried out a kind of ministry. "I've had a great life," he said. "I loved what I was doing, and I know for a fact that I brought something good to the ballpark. . . . [I] tried to make the world a little bit better by people's interactions with me." Reflecting on the interview, Heath admitted that he was taken aback by how much meaning Howard found peddling cold ones at the ballpark. "But I guess that's the point, right?" he said. "That you can make your job as big or small as you want. Here is the ultimate transactional job, the guy who walks the stairs and charges you $14 for a beer. And yet, he made something bigger from it." Howard was able to find the largeness in littleness.

Or I think of my mom. She has always been a loving and supportive presence for my dad and my brother and me, even if (as is too often the case with family) we have at times taken her for granted. She toiled for years as a med tech in the windowless basement laboratory of a hospital, examining human fluids under the flickering lights of fluorescent lamps. (It's as pleasant as it sounds.) But as she went about her work with a smile on her face and music on her lips, mom left a lasting imprint on her coworkers and everyone she met. I'll never forget one day visiting her at the lab, when one of those coworkers just shook her head and said to me, "There's no explaining the way your mama sings while she works down here, 'cept that she's got *the joy of Jesus*."

So as you reflect on your own next steps in the quiet ambition, think little and start where you are. The vision of the quiet ambition doesn't depend on a particular location or vocation. It doesn't require you to become a farmer if you are a banker or to move to the country if you're in the suburbs (though it doesn't rule it out, either). When I was called away recently from the pastoral life of my small-town parish to start teaching at our denomination's seminary, smack in the middle of a city, I was loath to leave; I cherished our quiet life. But a trusted mentor set me straight. He said, "It doesn't matter where you are or what you're doing, whether you're a parent or a pastor or a professor or whatever. All any of us can do is scratch away at our little corner of the kingdom and pray, Thy will be done. The battle is the Lord's."

So it is. Start therefore by imagining the quiet ambition simply at the scale of this week, right where you are. You begin with turning down the volume on some of the noisemakers in your life. You don't awake to anxiously check your smartphone—which is parked in another room, and in any case you've made it as "dumb" as possible.[14] Instead, you carve out your own "one square inch" of solitude in which you can, in the words of Father Greg Boyle, "marinate in the intimacy of God."[15] Maybe it's before anyone else wakes up, or maybe it's during your commute, turning off the radio for a moment of quiet communion with the Father, even as the cars around you are honking and harried. (Just because everyone else is in a rush doesn't mean you and I have to be too!) You've silently put a stake in the ground of your schedule.

Which is also why, when work encourages you to take on that extra project that could "look really good on your resume," or the kids' school is pressuring them to participate in yet another extracurricular activity, or friends are asking the family to dinner for what would be your fourth night away from home this week, you gently but firmly decline. Your calendar may be populated with dance recitals, get-togethers, all manner of happenings at church—good things for which you're grateful!—but you are also deliberate about building in room to rest and dwell in the rhythms of routine life. You can't quit your Martha streak, but you can do your level best to give Mary her due too. *I confess, I am not the Christ.*

There are countless things you *could* do today, but you recognize that what is most important are the particular good works—and good *work*—God has already prepared and put in your path. You'll take care of *this* customer, attend to *this* patient, help *this* student. Whether your livelihood entails a blue collar or a white; whether it's manual labor, management, or manning an office, you pray that God establishes the work of your hands. Neither Rome nor the kingdom of God is built in a day: you can only tend to your business on the day you're given. You'll also show loving labor on behalf of your neighbor—the "nearby guy"—and there are none nearer by than the family. And so where you have to stretch, you'll be like Mom in *The Incredibles* and stretch on behalf of them.

Others are taking notice as you live this way. You didn't realize that the mom whose oil you changed with a patient explanation for how to open the hood was having a no-good, very bad day, but you made it a bit better. The grumpy neighbor would never admit it, but he actually appreciates it when you smile and greet him as you walk the dog; almost no one else does that. Those words of encouragement you give your kids don't seem to make a difference, but they're depositing pennies in a bank of character and collecting interest. In all this you aren't opening the fire hose of the love of Jesus; you're walking gracefully and giving cups of cool water—all he ever called us to do.

When work is done, you occasionally wind down with the "telly-telly bunkum box," as Roald Dahl's BFG memorably called the TV, but more often you choose to do the hobby that few others know you enjoy: cross-stitching pillows or chopping wood or tinkering with model trains. Maybe you try your hand at baking a loaf of sourdough or play in the dirt of a small garden you've begun to tend—which, among the weeds, evidences a few bright bell peppers. Sometimes you even get that sensation that accompanies creation: *this is very good*. And when dinner doesn't look like something that would make the Food Network gush, you add a tad more butter, say grace, and break bread with glad and thankful hearts nevertheless.

You might not feel like Mother Teresa as you go about your week, but perhaps you start to carry yourself with a bit more of the easy grace of Saint Helen and her nickels. You forgive that remark from the next-door neighbor about the look of your lawn, extend a tad more patience helping your spouse with the housework, let one more person in line in front of you. You aren't applying for Human of the Year anytime soon, but then again you don't have to: the One who rose from the dead has given you all the notoriety you need. Your hope is built not on the sinking sand of your accomplishments but on the solid rock of his empty tomb. Who will help you count all these blessings?

Thinking little was also, in his own idiosyncratic way, the approach of our friend Henry David. Biographer Walter Harding recounts a moment late in Thoreau's life when his *modus vivendi* became clear. "The circle of his walks in Concord gradually narrowed," Harding writes. "Once he walked out to Flint's Bridge with [his friend Ellery] Channing. Speaking of some minute thing he had observed, he told him that *it was the art of genius to raise the little into the large* and Channing thought that a remarkably good summation of Thoreau's own best capabilities."[16]

This well characterizes Thoreau in his modest way, but much more so is it an apt description of what the Lord does for you and me. It is the art of his divine genius to raise our little into his large. We can find hope in the midst of the overlooked and undervalued stuff of everyday life because of the confidence that, in the sight of God now and in view of all creation on the last day, what might seem small is in truth gloriously, splendidly grand.

Have Need of Nothing

The Rose Bowl Parade couldn't hold a candle to this procession. Throngs of admirers lined the way: boys and girls, musicians innumerable, a whole menagerie of cats and dogs and horses and birds, and bright sprites scattering flowers and dancing for joy. In many ways, it's a procession like none on earth has ever seen. Not least because of the one in whose honor it is given.

C. S. Lewis paints the scene for us in his book *The Great Divorce*, which recounts one pilgrim's imagined field trip from hell to heaven. At the climax of the account, our pilgrim beholds this awesome paradisal parade. He's awestruck by the majesty and ceremony and can only wonder what grand hero could elicit such adoration, though he has his suspicions. Fumbling with his words, he whispers to his guide, "Is it? . . . is it?"

> "Not at all," said he. "It's someone ye'll never have heard of. Her name on Earth was Sarah Smith and she lived at Golders Green."
>
> "She seems to be . . . well, a person of particular importance?"
>
> "Aye. She is one of the great ones. Ye have heard that fame in this country and fame on Earth are two quite different things."[17]

Plainly Sarah Smith is someone who, on earth, neither captured nor commanded attention. Her very name is about as vanilla as it gets. And yet in heaven a grand procession is held in her honor. We learn that the crowd of children accompanying her are "her sons and daughters." Not due to having such a large biological family, but because "every young man or boy that met her became her son—even if it was only the boy that brought the meat to her back door. Every girl that met her was her daughter." Sarah Smith knew no strangers, especially among the least of these.

And all the animals? "Did she keep a sort of zoo?" the pilgrim asks. No, the guide explains: "Every beast and bird that came near her had its place in her love. In her they became themselves. And now the abundance of life she has in Christ from the Father flows over into them."

These are fine tributes, to be sure, but hardly anything warranting a parade in heaven, right? Sarah Smith of Golders Green is an obscure saint if ever there was one. She seems to have done no great things, accomplished no ambitious feats, won no laurels while on earth. But then this is just the point. "It is like when you throw a stone into a pool," explains the guide:

> And the concentric waves spread out further and further. Who knows where it will end? Redeemed humanity is still young, it has hardly come to its full strength. But already there is joy enough in the little finger of a great saint such as yonder lady to waken all the dead things of the universe into life.[18]

The story of Sarah Smith of Golders Green reminds us that the pathway of hope amid the everyday delights and disappointments of this mortal life need not appear on some grand scale. More often than not, it will look more like a widow's mite.

What's more, she brings us back to where we together began in our exploration of the quiet ambition. C. S. Lewis's imaginative narration is a faithful gloss on that verse from I Corinthians: "Be steadfast, immovable, always abounding in the work of the Lord, knowing that in the Lord your labor is not in vain" (1 Cor 15:58). As "redeemed humanity," we can lead quiet lives, tending our own business and working with our hands, confident that—when the last day comes—in Christ it is not for nothing.

And in him, we have need of nothing. There's one final phrase in the unambitious ambition of 1 Thessalonians 4:11-12 that we've neglected to this point but mustn't miss, for I think it ties the whole message together. Paul writes, "Make it your ambition to live quietly, tend your own business, and work with your hands, so that you walk gracefully toward outsiders *and have need of nothing*."

Don't sleep on that last little clause, "have need of nothing." Though sometimes translated "be dependent on no one," it's almost a direct echo of the Lord's words to Martha: she was "worried and anxious about many things," Jesus said, "but *there is need of one thing*. Mary has chosen the good portion, which will not be taken away from her" (Lk 10:42).[19]

The good portion is receiving from Jesus; the good portion is the Lord himself. As the late great Rich Mullins once sang, "Who have I in heaven but you, Jesus? And what better can I hope to find down here on earth? . . . There's a world but I'd just be wasting my time . . . you're my one thing."[20] Martha had need of but one thing: the Lord Jesus. And we do too.

The quiet ambition, far from being a program of self-reliance, is a counsel of Christ-reliance. As we live quietly, we lean on Christ in the little things of everyday life. We look to him to be the glue that holds together this patched-up kindergarten craft that we call life. He's the One, the only One, who can do it. But when we have the one thing, we have need of nothing, and that is no little thing.

ACKNOWLEDGMENTS

QUIET LIVES OF HOPE are only possible in the context of community. Countless people have given me a deepening appreciation for what it means to live quietly, and—in ways both direct and indirect—contributed to the composition of this book.

First and foremost I am grateful to my wife, Anne, and our children Samuel, Louis, Beatrice, and Elisabeth. Each and every day they encourage, inspire, and challenge me in our shared adventure of the quiet ambition. This book could not have been written without them; without them, I probably would not have *wanted* to write it. I'm thankful, too, for my in-laws, Pete and Cindy, who have been cheerleaders throughout this project (and not only then!); it was at their peaceful cabin in Colorado that the idea first took shape.

Many friends have spurred me on in my writing over the years. Jason, Tony, Adam, Jim, Chris, Mike, Scott, and Josh: thank you for being some of my first readers and ever-faithful friends. To my Hook & Line guys—Joel, Chip, Billy, John, Travis, and Mike—your companionship in the journey of faith has been a gift. Next year in Idaho! Tanner Olson speaks into my life as only a fellow writer can. Apart from the urging and the connections of Dave Zahl this book probably doesn't get published; I'm deeply grateful for his generous aid.

Alexander Field at the Bindery took a chance on a country pastor who had an idea and a couple of thousand words. His belief helped propel this project forward. So, too, did the thoughtful critiques and reassurance of my editor, Kelli Trujillo. Her input not only improved the manuscript; it has helped me grow as a person.

This book was largely forged in my years of parish ministry, and the congregations that I have been privileged to serve have shaped my faith and my writing. Great thanks and admiration are due the saints of Faith Lutheran Church in Seaside, California, and Beautiful Savior Lutheran Church in Spokane, Washington. God's people of Trinity Lutheran Church in Arcadia, Michigan, will always have a special place in my heart. Thank you for your patient love and support for this unsteady under-shepherd. I am honored now to serve alongside the faculty of Concordia Seminary and to teach our earnest and faithful students. It is a joy and privilege to be in their midst.

Finally, I am profoundly grateful for my brother, Peter, and my parents, Patrick and Patrice. Their unfailing support, curiosity, and encouragement have helped to make me the writer and man that I am. I wish to express especial gratitude to my mom. She showed me what it meant to be a quiet saint before I had words for it. To her this book is dedicated.

NOTES

Preface

[1]This has some resonance and overlap with the two groups Alan Noble designates as the Affirming and the Resigned in his book *You Are Not Your Own* (Downers Grove, IL: InterVarsity Press, 2021). Whereas Noble focuses more on identity and belonging, this book focuses on purpose and vocation.

[2]This is my own translation. I'll give it more (much more) context as we go throughout the course of the book.

[3]Douglas McKelvey, *Every Moment Holy, Volume 1* (Nashville: Rabbit Room Press, 2017), © 2017 by Douglas Kaine McKelvey, used with permission.

[4]McKelvey, *Every Moment Holy*, 201.

[5]McKelvey, *Every Moment Holy*, 202.

[6]McKelvey, *Every Moment Holy*, 206.

1. Escaping Quiet Desperation

[1]His third day at Walden, Henry David Thoreau wrote in his journal: "I wish to meet the facts of life—the vital facts, which are the phenomena or actuality the gods meant to show us—face to face, and so I came down here. Life! Who knows what it is, what it does?" Quoted in Jeffrey Cramer, *Walden: A Fully Annotated Edition* (New Haven, CT: Yale University Press, 2004), xviii.

[2]Cramer, *Walden: A Fully Annotated Edition*, 91.

[3]Michael Sims, *The Adventures of Henry Thoreau* (New York: Bloomsbury, 2014), 164.

[4]Henry David Thoreau, *Walden*, Oxford World Classics (Oxford: Oxford University Press, 1997), 83. Authors John Kaag and Jonathan Van Belle write in their book *Henry at Work*, "Workdays come and go, time passes on, and it is so easy to let it pass you by without making a meaningful mark. Henry, the

consummate worker, the one we look to in understanding the meaning of work, often fretted about its potential worthlessness. We suspect that this fretting is at least in part what kept him on the move." John Kaag and Jonathan Van Belle, *Henry at Work* (Princeton, NJ: Princeton University Press, 2023), 84.

[5]Ken Burns, producer, "Walden Film," 17:25 (2017, Walden Woods Project), accessed March 12, 2024, www.walden.org/walden-film/.

[6]Thoreau, *Walden*, 9.

[7]C. S. Lewis, *The Screwtape Letters* (San Francisco: Harper, 2001), 61.

[8]Thoreau, *Walden*, 48.

[9]Lin-Manuel Miranda, *Hamilton: An American Musical.*

[10]*Conan O'Brien Can't Stop*, directed by Rodman Flender (New York: Magnolia Pictures, 2011).

[11]Malcolm Gladwell, "Blame Game," *Revisionist History,* accessed March 12, 2025, www.pushkin.fm/podcasts/revisionist-history/blame-game.

[12]Erin Griffith, "Why Are Young People Pretending to Love Work?" *New York Times,* January 26, 2019.

[13]Timothy Leary, *Turn On, Tune In, Drop Out*, sixth edition (Berkeley, CA: Ronin Publishing, 2024).

[14]Jim Harter, "Is Quiet Quitting Real?" Gallup.com, September 6, 2022, www.gallup.com/workplace/398306/quiet-quitting-real.aspx.

[15]The term was coined by Derek Thompson in his seminal essay for *The Atlantic,* "Workism Is Making Americans Miserable," February 24, 2019, www.theatlantic.com/ideas/archive/2019/02/religion-workism-making-americans-miserable/583441. Interestingly, Thompson's thesis is that, for many Americans, "Work has morphed into a religious identity."

[16]Arianna Huffington, "Quiet Quitting Isn't Just About Quitting on a Job," LinkedIn, accessed August 7, 2024, www.linkedin.com/posts/ariannahuffington_joyfuljoining-work-culture-activity-6965397668625805312-wsOR.

[17]Anthony Bradley, *Heroic Fraternities* (Eugene, OR: Wipf & Stock, 2023), 82.

[18]"All Depends on Our Possessing," translated by Catherine Winkworth, *Lutheran Service Book* (St. Louis: CPH, 2006), 732.

[19]John Piper, *Don't Waste Your Life* (Wheaton, IL: Crossway, 2003).

[20]Robert Frost, "Two Tramps in Mud Time" in *The Poetry of Robert Frost,* edited by Edward Connery Lathem (Henry Holt and Company, 1969), 275.

[21]Philip Yancey, *Disappointment with God* (Grand Rapids, MI: Zondervan, 1988), 9.

[22]Oliver Burkeman, *4,000 Weeks* (New York: Picador, 2021), 208. His soft nihilism aside, Burkeman's book has much to offer in giving a proper

appreciation for "time management." Inasmuch as it's a kind of modern *memento mori*, it's salutary medicine. He comes up short on offering ultimate hope, but perhaps he's not far from the kingdom.

[23]Yancey, *Disappointment with God*, 24.

[24]George Eliot, *George Eliot's Life*, vol. 1, chap. 1, accessed March 12, 2025, www.gutenberg.org/files/43043/43043-h/43043-h.htm.

[25]Chad Bird first drew my attention to this in his book *Upside-Down Spirituality* (Grand Rapids, MI: Brazos, 2019).

[26]*Seinfeld*, television sitcom created by Jerry Seinfeld and Larry David, NBC, 1989–1998.

2. Making a Name

[1]F. Scott Fitzgerald, *The Great Gatsby* (New York: Scribner, 1925), 98.

[2]Augustine of Hippo, *Tractates on the Gospel of John* 6.10.2, quoted in Andrew Louth, ed., *Genesis 1–11*, Ancient Christian Commentary on Scripture (Downers Grove, IL: InterVarsity Press, 2001), 167.

[3]John Chrysostom, *Homilies on Genesis 30.5*, quoted in Louth, *Genesis 1–11*, 167.

[4]Martin Luther, *Luther's Commentary on Genesis I* (Grand Rapids, MI: Zondervan, 1958), 192. For an interpretation that views "making a name" in more neutral, or even positive, terms, see John Walton, "Beware Our Tower of Babel," *Christianity Today*, March 2023.

[5]Formed as a compound from a pair of significant Greek words, *philos* (a dear one, a friend) and *timē* (honor). There is an interesting secular analogy with what management guru Jim Collins calls "Level 5 Leadership" in his best-seller *Good to Great* (New York: HarperCollins, 2001): "[Level 5 Leaders] are incredibly ambitious—but their ambition is first and foremost for the institution, not themselves" (21).

[6]Craig Hill, *Servant of All* (Grand Rapids, MI: Eerdmans, 2016), 150. Note that the New Testament does use a second term for *ambition* that is unambiguously negative. *Eritheia* (which appears in Rom 2:8; 2 Cor 12:20; Gal 5:20; Phil 1:17; 2:3; and Jas 3:14, 16) is typically translated as "selfish ambition." It's the self-seeking, grasping, clawing, climbing variation. Traditionally, it was translated simply as "ambition." As theologian Michael Horton has pointed out, only recently has society sufficiently whitewashed the conventional notion of ambition that a modifier is now needed to make clear whether it is intended negatively. See Michael Horton, *Ordinary* (Grand Rapids, MI: Zondervan, 2014).

[7]Katelyn Beaty, *Celebrities for Jesus* (Grand Rapids, MI: Brazos, 2022).

[8]I do not mean to suggest that was the only issue at play. In the case of these men in particular there are a host of other issues that go beyond the purview of our discussion here.

[9]Beaty, *Celebrities for Jesus*, 73.

[10]Note the quick pivot from popularity to pointed assertion: "Now great crowds accompanied him, and he turned and said to them, 'If anyone comes to me and does not hate his own father and mother and wife and children and brothers and sisters, yes, and even his own life, he cannot be my disciple'" (Lk 14:25-26).

[11]Anonymous, "What Wondrous Love Is This," 1811, public domain.

[12]See especially Romans 6:3-4, Titus 3:5, and 1 Peter 3:21, alongside Jesus' preferential option for the youngest among us (Lk 18:15-17).

[13]Wendell Berry, *A Timbered Choir* (Berkeley, CA: Counterpoint, 1998), 18.

3. Noisemakers

[1]Brian Tallerico, "A Quiet Place: Review," RogerEbert.com, April 6, 2018, www.rogerebert.com/reviews/a-quiet-place-2018.

[2]Nate Silver, *The Signal and the Noise* (New York: Penguin, 2012), 17.

[3]Gordon Hempton, *One Square Inch of Silence* (New York: Free Press, 2009), 13.

[4]Ken Myers, "Interview with Arthur Boers," Mars Hill Audio, 113:3.

[5]John Mark Comer, *The Ruthless Elimination of Hurry* (New York: Waterbrook, 2019), 19.

[6]Homer, *The Odyssey*, book 12.

[7]For those who are looking for more concrete advice on taking steps in this direction, I recommend Andy Crouch, *The Tech-Wise Family* (Grand Rapids, MI: Baker, 2017) and Cal Newport, *Digital Minimalism* (New York: Penguin, 2019).

[8]Olivia Reingold, "The Parents Saying No to Smartphones," *The Free Press*, May 22, 2023, thefp.com/p/the-parents-saying-no-to-smartphones.

[9]Jonathan Haidt and Zach Rausch, "Kids Who Get Smartphones Earlier Become Adults with Worse Mental Health," *After Babel*, May 15, 2023, www.afterbabel.com/p/sapien-smartphone-report. See also Jonathan Haidt, *The Anxious Generation* (New York: Penguin, 2024).

[10]Tricia McCary Rhodes, *The Wired Soul* (Colorado Springs, CO: NavPress, 2016).

[11]Saint Augustine, *Confessions*, book 1.

[12]Keith Richards and Mick Jagger, "(I Can't Get No) Satisfaction," *(I Can't Get No) Satisfaction* (Hollywood, CA: RCA 1965).

[13]Rich Mullins, "My One Thing," *Never Picture Perfect* (Brentwood, TN: Reunion, 1989).

[14]Michael Gerson, "Sunday Sermon by Michael Gerson," Washington National Cathedral, February 17, 2019, https://youtu.be/xYu4xKGRi8Q.

[15]David Brooks, *How to Know a Person* (New York: Random House, 2023), 128.

[16]Hempton, *One Square Inch,* 216.

[17]C. S. Lewis, "The Weight of Glory," in *The Weight of Glory and Other Addresses* (San Francisco: HarperCollins, 2001).

4. Quiet Saints

[1]Abraham J. Malherbe, *The Letters to the Thessalonians* (New Haven, CT: Yale University Press, 2000), 247.

[2]Seneca, *Epistles* 68 §10.

[3]Malherbe, *Letters to the Thessalonians,* 247.

[4]Mitch Albom, "Quietly Flying High, Lions Running Back Has Learned to Absorb and Endure," *Detroit Free Press,* November 21, 2008, www.mitchalbom.com/101barry-sanders-quietly-flying-highlions-running-back-has-learned-absorb-and-endure.

[5]M. B. Roberts, "Sanders' Humility Makes Him Distinctive," www.espn.com/classic/biography/s/Sanders_Barry.html.

[6]Albom, "Quietly Flying High."

[7]Barry Sanders, *Bye Bye Barry* (Beverly Hills, CA: Mission Matters, 2023), 115.

[8]Albom, "Quietly Flying High."

[9]*Bye Bye Barry,* directed by Paul Monusky, Micaela Powers, and Angela Torma (NFL Films, 2023).

[10]J. R. R. Tolkien, *The Fellowship of the Ring* (Boston: Houghton Mifflin, 1965), 10.

[11]Tolkien, *Fellowship of the Ring,* 11.

[12]See Christopher Snyder, *Hobbit Virtues* (New York: Pegasus, 2020), especially chap. 5.

[13]Josef Pieper, *In Tune with the World* (South Bend, IN: St. Augustine's Press, 1999).

[14]Tolkien, *Fellowship of the Ring,* 11.

[15]Alexander Schmemann, *For the Life of the World* (Crestwood, NY: St. Vladimir's Press, 1963), 16.

[16]Jack Shoemaker, ed., *What I Stand On: The Collected Essays of Wendell Berry 1969–2017* (New York: Library of America, 2019).

[17]J. R. R. Tolkien, *The Return of the King* (Boston: Houghton Mifflin, 1955), book 6, chap. 8.

[18]Ben Sasse, *Them* (New York: St. Martin's Press), 213.

[19]Sasse, *Them,* 217.

[20]Rosa Parks, *Quiet Strength* (Grand Rapids, MI: Zondervan, 1994), 70.

[21]Parks, *Quiet Strength,* 71.

[22]Park, *Quiet Strength,* 77.

[23]Susan Cain, *Quiet* (New York: Crown, 2012), 2.

[24]Harry Emerson Fosdick, "God of Grace and God of Glory," 1930, public domain.

[25]James Bryan Smith, *An Arrow Pointing to Heaven* (Nashville: B&H, 2000), 171.

[26]Smith, *Arrow Pointing to Heaven,* 149.

[27]*Rich Mullins: A Ragamuffin's Legacy,* directed by David Leo (Los Angeles, CA: Color Green Films, 2015).

[28]Rich Mullins, "Telling the Joke," in *The World As I Remember It* (Portland, OR: Multnomah, 2004), 26.

[29]Mullins, "Telling the Joke," 27.

[30]Warner Sallman, *Head of Christ*, 1940, oil, Warner Sallman Collection, Anderson University, Indiana, https://anderson.edu/galleries/warner-sallman/.

[31]Thomas O. Chisholm, "Great Is Thy Faithfulness," 1923, public domain.

5. The Blasphemous Anxiety

[1]Quoted in Eugene Peterson, *The Contemplative Pastor* (Grand Rapids, MI: Eerdmans, 1989), 17–18.

[2]I by no means wish to impugn a faithful disciple of our Lord who, as John shows in his Gospel, was a devoted follower and dear friend (see Jn 11). But for that same reason I like to think that Martha would recognize and receive this critique—which, in any case, will be further complicated presently: she is clearly not the only guilty party in the biblical accounts.

[3]Brandon Warmke and Justin Tosi, *Why It's Okay to Mind Your Own Business* (New York: Routledge, 2024).

[4]Warmke and Tosi, *Why It's Okay*, 16.

[5]Plato, *Republic*, 433a. Quoted in Warmke and Tosi, *Why It's Okay*, 37.

[6]John Milton, *Paradise Lost* 1.254-263.

[7]Ben Quash and Michael Ward, eds., *Heresies and How to Avoid Them* (Grand Rapids, MI: Baker Academic, 2007), 88.

[8]Hal Runkel, *Scream-Free Parenting* (New York: Broadway Books, 2007), 31.

[9]Brett McKay, host, *Art of Manliness*, podcast, episode 489, "How to Get a Handle on Your Anger" with guest David Lieberman, Get Action: Art of Manliness, September 30, 2021, www.artofmanliness.com/character/behavior/how-to-deal-with-anger.

[10]C. S. Lewis, *The Voyage of the Dawn Treader* (San Francisco: Harper, 1994), 248. See also Lewis's comments on pride ("the great sin") in *Mere Christianity* (San Francisco: Harper, 2001), 122.

[11]Lest Peter get too big of a head, Jesus makes sure to let him know that "flesh and blood did not reveal this to you, but my Father in heaven" (Mt 16:17 CSB). In other words, don't get cocky, pal. Even this recognition is a gift. So too for us.

[12]Dietrich Bonhoeffer, *Life Together* (San Francisco: Harper, 1954), 27.

[13]Will Mancini, *God Dreams* (Nashville: B&H, 2016).

[14]Bonhoeffer, *Life Together*, 28.

[15]For an authoritative discussion of the possible motivations for Judas's betrayal, see Raymond E. Brown, *The Death of the Messiah* (New Haven, CT: Yale University Press, 1998), 1394-1418.

6. God's Business and Ours

[1]I'm not here to adjudicate whether or not Thomas and Ulrich make it in; I wouldn't be tending my own business.

[2]Paul Zahl, *Grace in Practice* (Grand Rapids, MI: Eerdmans, 2007).

[3]Augustus Toplady, "Rock of Ages," 1776, public domain.

[4]Bo Giertz, *The Hammer of God* (Minneapolis: Augsburg, 1955), 123.

[5]Chad Bird, *Upside-Down Spirituality* (Grand Rapids, MI: Brazos, 2019), 54.

[6]Greg is a guy who gets God's business. Check out his book *Joining Jesus on His Mission* (Tyler, TX: Tenth Power, 2014).

[7]Jon Tyson, "Kids, Not Kings," email newsletter, August 10, 2022.

[8]Interestingly, the context for this quote was Luther writing to his beloved wife, Katie, who was herself in a fit of the blasphemous anxiety. The letter with its original source is found in Eric Gritsch, *The Wit of Martin Luther* (Minneapolis: Fortress, 2006), 64.

7. Polishing Forks for the Kingdom

[1]James Boswell, *Life of Johnson* (Oxford: Oxford University Press, 1998), 708.

[2]Abraham J. Malherbe, *The Letters to the Thessalonians* (New Haven, CT: Yale University Press), 250.

[3]Aristotle, *Metaphysics* 1.1.

[4]In recent years this has been especially brought to Americans' attention through the work of television personality and podcast host Mike Rowe through his Discovery Channel show *Dirty Jobs* and his foundation Mike Rowe Works, https://mikeroweworks.org/.

[5]"Jobber's Blue-Collar Report: Gen Z and the Uncertain Future of the Trades," Jobber, 2023, accessed February 9, 2025, https://getjobber.com/bluecollar report.

[6]Brian Dijkema, "The Work of Our Hands," *Cardus,* spring 2015.

[7]Wendell Berry, *A Timbered Choir* (Washington, DC: Counterpoint, 1998), 18.

[8]Leo Tolstoy, *Anna Karenina* (Oxford: Oxford University Press, 2008), 252, emphasis added.

[9]The last couple decades or so have seen a flood of interest in the topic of vocation or, as it's sometimes called, "faith and work." Books by Gene Veith, Os Guinness, Tim Keller, and others are gradually shifting the narrative.

[10]On the limitations of the pursuit of passions, see Cal Newport, *So Good They Can't Ignore You* (New York: Hachette, 2012).

[11]For the history of the doctrine of vocation's development, see especially Gustav Wingren, *Luther on Vocation* (Eugene, OR: Wipf & Stock, 2004).

[12]Martin Luther, "Exposition of Psalm 147," in *Luther's Works* 14 (St. Louis: Concordia Publishing House, 1958), emphasis added.

[13]Gene Edward Veith, *God at Work* (Wheaton, IL: Crossway, 2002), 17.

[14]Matthew Crawford, in his excellent book on the value of manual labor, *Shop Class as Soulcraft* (New York: Penguin, 2009), is even more blunt: "While manufacturing jobs have certainly left our shores to a disturbing degree, the manual trades have not. If you need a deck built, or your car fixed, the Chinese are of no help. Because they are in China."

[15]Martin Luther, *Luther's Works* 45 (Minneapolis: Fortress, 1962), 39-40. Note well that Luther assumes that it is the *dad* who is changing the diapers!

[16]David Guzik, "Study Guide for 1 Thessalonians 4," accessed March 13, 2025, www.blueletterbible.org/comm/guzik_david/study-guide/1-thessalonians/1-thessalonians-4.cfm.

[17]Tish Harrison Warren, *The Liturgy of the Ordinary* (Downers Grove, IL: InterVarsity Press, 2016), 22.

[18]*The Bear*, "Forks," directed by Christopher Storer, June 22, 2023, on Hulu.

8. The Need to Knead

[1]"About," on Etsy website, accessed March 13, 2025, www.etsy.com/about.

[2]Oxford English Dictionary, s.v. "'to work with one's hands' in hand (n.), sense P.2.r," accessed February 9, 2025, https://doi.org/10.1093/OED/2565452112.

[3]Oxford English Dictionary, s.v. "handiwork (n.), sense 1," accessed February 9, 2025, https://doi.org/10.1093/OED/7707122124.

[4]Rick Rubin, *The Creative Act: A Way of Being* (New York: Penguin, 2023), 3.

[5]It should also be noted that one of the ways the capacity for creativity can be corrupted is through idolatry. The phrase "the work of human hands" in the Scriptures even becomes a byword for false gods (e.g., Deut 4:28; Ps 115:4; Is 44:9).

[6]Arthur Boers, *Living into Focus* (Grand Rapids, MI: Brazos, 2012), 10.

[7]Rubin, *Creative Act*, 1.

[8]*WALL-E*, directed by Andrew Stanton (Emeryville, CA: Disney Pixar, 2008).

[9]Doug Stowe, *The Wisdom of Our Hands* (Fresno, CA: Linden, 2022), 24.

[10]Stowe, *Wisdom of Our Hands*, 125.

[11]Wendell Berry, "The Pleasures of Eating," in *What Are People For?* (New York: North Point Press, 1990), 146.

[12]Along these lines, King Arthur Baking Co. reported that it sold more than 156 million pounds of flour in 2020, as sales rose 61 percent over the year before, in Ellen Byron, "Is Baking's Pandemic Popularity Just a Flash in the Pan?" *The Wall Street Journal,* May 25, 2021, www.wsj.com/articles/is-bakings-pandemic-popularity-just-a-flash-in-the-pan-11621951200.

[13]Grace Randall, "Baking Boom Is Over for Burnt Out Home Cooks," AHDB.org, November 17, 2021, https://ahdb.org.uk/news/consumer-insight-baking-boom-is-over-for-burnt-out-home-cooks.

[14]Peter Reinhart, *The Bread Baker's Apprentice* (Berkeley, CA: Ten Speed Press, 2001), 59.

[15]In his book *4,000 Weeks*, Oliver Burkeman introduced me to the delightful German term *eigenzeit*, which is roughly translated as "the time inherent to the process itself" (New York: Picador, 2021, 33).

[16]For the following reflections, I am indebted to Peter Reinhart, especially his book *The Bread Baker's Apprentice* and his interview with Ken Myers in the Mars Hill Audio journal conversation, "Bread and the Hungry Soul," April 1, 1995, https://mha-members.org/conversations/bread-and-the-hungry-soul/.

[17]J. R. R. Tolkien, "On Fairy-Stories." The essay is available in the public domain at several sites online, including https://coolcalvary.com/wp-content/uploads/2018/10/on-fairy-stories1.pdf, accessed March 13, 2025.

[18]See Cal Newport, *Digital Minimalism* (New York: Penguin, 2019), 59-84.

9. Mustard Seed Missionaries and Coffee Bean Christians

[1]Andy Crouch, *Culture Making* (Downers Grove, IL: InterVarsity Press, 2009).

[2]Abraham J. Malherbe, *The Letters to the Thessalonians* (New Haven, CT: Yale University Press, 2000), 251.

[3]David Zahl, *Low Anthropology* (Grand Rapids, MI: Brazos, 2022), 17.

[4]Crouch, *Culture Making*, 200.

[5]Crouch, *Culture Making*, 201.

[6]Josh White, "Making Haste Slowly in Our Walk with God," *Christianity Today*, accessed July 26, 2024, www.christianitytoday.com/ct/2023/april-web-only/josh-white-stumbling-toward-eternity-make-haste-slowly-god.html.

[7]Kosuke Koyama, *Three Mile an Hour God* (London: SCM Press, 2021).

[8]"Goodspeed," produced by Danny Lund, accessed March 13, 2025, www.livegodspeed.org/watchgodspeed.

[9]Jon Gordon, *The Coffee Bean* (Hoboken, NJ: Wiley, 2019), 24.

[10]James Davison Hunter, *To Change the World* (Oxford: Oxford University Press, 2010).

[11]Greg Thompson, "The Church in Our Time: Nurturing Congregations of Faithful Presence," Flourish Collective, accessed July 10, 2024, www.flourishcollective.org/academy/wp-content/uploads/The-Church-In-Our-Time-A-New-City-Commons-White-Paper_4.pdf.

[12]Hunter, *To Change the World*, 241.

[13]I first heard this phrase in the title of a book by author Tom Sine, *The Mustard Seed Conspiracy* (Waco, TX: Word, 1981).

[14]Greg Finke, *Joining Jesus on His Mission* (Tyler, TX: Tenth Power, 2013).

[15]Leah Libresco, *Building the Benedict Option* (San Francisco: Ignatius, 2018), 22.

[16]Mike Aquilina, "The Salt of the Empire," *Touchstone Magazine*, May 2004.

[17]Amor Towles, *A Gentleman in Moscow* (New York: Penguin, 2016), 316.

[18]Peter Berger, "The Good of Religious Pluralism," *First Things*, April 2016.

10. Them That Are Without

[1]Lesslie Newbigin, *The Open Secret* (Grand Rapids, MI: Eerdmans, 1995), 32.

[2]Aaron Renn, *Life in the Negative World* (Grand Rapids, MI: Zondervan, 2024). See also Rod Dreher, *The Benedict Option* (New York: Sentinel, 2017). The echo of Dreher's book in the aforementioned Jonah option notwithstanding, I'm sympathetic to Dreher's concerns and appreciate many of his constructive recommendations.

[3]In case you don't have the foggiest idea what I'm talking about, *The Outsiders* is a coming-of-age novel by S. E. Hinton that I read in middle school (New York: Viking Press, 1967). It was adapted for film in 1983, starring Emilio Estevez, Matt Dillon, Ralph Macchio, and others who had come affectionately to be known as the "Brat Pack."

[4]Robert Farrar Capon, *Kingdom, Grace, Judgment* (Grand Rapids, MI: Eerdmans, 2002).

[5]Dietrich Bonhoeffer, *Discipleship: Dietrich Bonhoeffer Works* (Minneapolis: Fortress, 2003), 4:48.

[6]Charles Marsh, *Strange Glory: A Life of Dietrich Bonhoeffer* (New York: Knopf, 2014), 199.

[7]Marsh, *Strange Glory*, 196.

[8]Dietrich Bonhoeffer, *Dietrich Bonhoeffer Works, Volume 13: London 1933–1935* (Minneapolis: Fortress, 2007), 217.

[9]Bonhoeffer, *London 1933–1935*, 39-41.

[10]Bonhoeffer, *London 1933–1935*, 349-53 (emphasis added).

[11]Bonhoeffer would in fact leave Germany on another occasion, this time for the United States in 1939. But it wouldn't take him two years to make up his mind to return that time. No sooner did he set foot in the United States then he got a ticket for a return trip to Germany.

[12]Frederick Buechner, *Wishful Thinking* (San Francisco: Harper & Row, 1973), 95.

[13]Thanks to my friend Jenny Anne Mannan for helping me to articulate these thoughts. See her thoughtful commencement address, "The Real Story of

Your Life," Mockingbird, May 24, 2024, https://mbird.com/everyday/the-real-story-of-your-life.

Conclusion: Think Little

[1]Biographical details for this section drawn from Richard Lischer's essay about Thérèse, "The Little Way," in *Our Hearts Are Restless* (Oxford: Oxford University Press, 2023), 209-24.

[2]Lischer, "The Little Way," 219.

[3]Lischer, "The Little Way," 224.

[4]Mother Teresa, *Mother Teresa: In My Own Words* (Liguori, MO: Liguori, 1997), 45.

[5]Michael Lewis, *Going Infinite* (New York: W.W. Norton, 2023), xv.

[6]Lewis, *Going Infinite*, xiv.

[7]Lewis, *Going Infinite*, 33.

[8]David Yaffee-Bellany and J. Edward Moreno, "Sam Bankman-Fried Sentenced to 25 Years in Prison," *The New York Times*, March 28, 2024.

[9]Lewis, *Going Infinite*, 138.

[10]Chad Bird, *Upside-Down Spirituality* (Grand Rapids, MI: Brazos, 2019), 184.

[11]Wendell Berry, "Think Little"; reprinted in *Think Little: Essays (Counterpoints)* (Berkeley, CA: Counterpoint, 2019), 19.

[12]*It's a Wonderful Life*, directed by Frank Capra (Los Angeles, CA: RKO Radio Pictures, 1946).

[13]Dan Heath, host, *What It's Like to Be*, podcast, season 1, episode 1, "A Stadium Beer Vendor," October 15, 2023, www.whatitsliketobe.com/2246914/episodes/13768110-a-stadium-beer-vendor.

[14]There are lots of hacks for doing this now. See, for instance, Doug Aamoth, "The Ultimate Focus Secret," Fast Company, July 9, 2019, www.fastcompany.com/90373183/the-ultimate-focus-secret-turn-your-smartphone-into-a-dumb-phone. And don't rule out ditching the smartphone altogether. Options like the Light Phone (www.thelightphone.com), which I use, are increasingly available.

[15]Greg Boyle, *Tattoos on the Heart* (New York: Free Press, 2010), 22.

[16]Walter Harding, *The Days of Henry Thoreau* (New York: Dover, 1962), 454, emphasis added.

[17]C. S. Lewis, *The Great Divorce* (London: Geoffrey Bies, 1945), chap. 12.

[18]Lewis, *The Great Divorce*, chap. 12.

[19]The Greek of 1 Thessalonians is *medenos chreian echete*, and in Luke it's *henos estin chreia*. I cannot say for certain that the echo is deliberate, but it is nevertheless unmistakable. When I encounter such instances in my study of the Bible, I remember that the human authors of Scripture are finally reliant on the divine Author and the inspiration of the Holy Spirit.

[20]Rich Mullins, "My One Thing," *Never Picture Perfect* (Brentwood, TN: Reunion, 1989).

BECOMING OUR TRUE SELVES

The nautilus is one of the sea's oldest creatures. Beginning with a tight center, its remarkable growth pattern can be seen in the ever-enlarging chambers that spiral outward. The nautilus in the IVP Formatio logo symbolizes deep inward work of spiritual formation that begins rooted in our souls and then opens to the world as we experience spiritual transformation. The shell takes on a stunning pearlized appearance as it ages and forms in much the same way as the souls of those who devote themselves to spiritual practice. Formatio books draw on the ancient wisdom of the saints and the early church as well as the rich resources of Scripture, applying tradition to the needs of contemporary life and practice.

Within each of us is a longing to be in God's presence. Formatio books call us into our deepest desires and help us to become our true selves in the light of God's grace.